Wyoming Laws

School Laws of Wyoming

in Force 1895

Wyoming Laws

School Laws of Wyoming
in Force 1895

ISBN/EAN: 9783337776091

Printed in Europe, USA, Canada, Australia, Japan

Cover: Foto ©Suzi / pixelio.de

More available books at **www.hansebooks.com**

SCHOOL LAWS

OF THE

STATE OF WYOMING

IN FORCE MARCH 31, 1895.

COMPILED BY ESTELLE REEL,
STATE SUPERINTENDENT OF PUBLIC INSTRUCTION,
CHEYENNE, WYOMING.

CHEYENNE, WYO.,
SUN-LEADER BOOK PUBLISHING HOUSE,
1895.

SCHOOL LAWS

STATE OF WYOMING.

(From the Act of Admission of the State of Wyoming, approved July 10, 1890)

(EXTRACT.)

*   *   *   *   *

GRANT OF SCHOOL LANDS.

Sec. 4. That sections numbered 16 and 36 in every township of said proposed State, and, where such sections, or any parts thereof, have been sold or otherwise disposed of by or under the authority of any act of Congress, other lands equivalent thereto, in legal sub-divisions of not less than one quarter section, and as contiguous as may be to the section in lieu of which the same is taken, are hereby granted to said State for the support of common schools, such indemnity lands to be selected within said State in such manner as the Legislature may provide, with the approval of the Secretary of the Interior; Provided, That Section 6 of the act of Congress of August 9, 1888, entitled, "An act to authorize the leasing of the school and university lands in the Territory of Wyoming, and for other purposes," shall apply to the school and university indemnity lands of the said State of Wyoming, so far as applicable

DISPOSAL OF GRANTED LANDS.

Sec. 5. That all lands herein granted for educational purposes shall be disposed of only at public sale, the proceeds to constitute a permanent school fund, the interest of which only shall be expended in the support of said schools. But said lands may, under such regulations as the Legislature shall prescribe, be leased for periods of not more than five years, in quantities not exceeding one section to any one person or company; and such land shall not be subject to pre-emption, homestead entry, or any other entry under the land laws of the United States, whether surveyed or unsurveyed, but shall be reserved for school purposes only.

*   *   *   *   *

PROCEEDS OF U. S. LAND SALE, PERCENTAGE TO STATE.

Sec. 7. That 5 per cent. of the proceeds of the sales of public lands lying within said State which shall be sold by the United States subsequent to the admission of said State into the Union, after deducting all expenses incident to the same, shall be paid to the said State, to be used as a permanent fund, the interest of which only shall be expended for the support of the common schools within said State.

LANDS GRANTED FOR SCHOOL PURPOSES.

Sec. 8. That the lands granted to the Territory of Wyoming by the act of February 18, 1881, entitled, "An act to grant lands to Dakota, Montana, Arizona, Idaho and Wyoming, for university purposes," are hereby vested in the State of Wyoming, to the extent of the full quantity of seventy-two sections to said State, and any portion of said lands that may not have been selected by said Territory of Wyoming may be selected by the said State; but said act of February 18, 1881, should be so amended as to provide that none of said lands shall be sold for less than $10 per acre, and the proceeds shall constitute a permanent fund to be safely invested and held by said State, and the income thereof be used exclusively for university purposes. The schools, colleges and universities provided for in this act shall forever remain under the exclusive control of the said State, and no part of the proceeds arising from the sale or disposal of any lands herein granted for educational purposes shall be used for the support of any sectarian or denominational school, college or university.

*   *   *   *   *

AGRICULTURAL LANDS.

Sec. 10. That 90,000 acres of land, to be selected and located as provided in Section 4 of this act, are hereby granted to said State for the use and support of an Agricultural College in said State, as provided in the acts of Congress making donations of lands for such purposes.

*   *   *   *   *

MINERAL LANDS EXCEPTED FROM GRANTS.

Sec. 13. That all mineral lands shall be exempted from the grants made by this act. But if Sections 16 and 36, or any sub-division or portion of any smallest sub division thereof in any township, shall be found by the Department of the Interior to be mineral lands, said State is hereby authorized and empowered to select, in legal sub-divisions, an equal quantity of other unappropriated lands in said State in lieu thereof, for the use and the benefit of the common schools of said State.

SELECTION OF LANDS.

Sec. 14. That all lands granted in quantity or as indemnity by this act, shall be selected, under the direction of the Secretary of the Interior, from the surveyed, unsurveyed and unappropriated public lands of the United States within the limits of the State entitled thereto. And there shall be deducted from the number of acres of land donated by this act for specific objects to said State, the number of acres heretofore donated by Congress to said Territory for similar objects.

CONSTITUTION.

ARTICLE IV.

EXECUTIVE DEPARTMENT.

(EXTRACT.)

* * * * *

PROVIDING FOR ELECTION OF STATE OFFICERS, INCLUDING A SUPERINTENDENT OF PUBLIC INSTRUCTION.

Sec. 11. There shall be chosen by the qualified electors of the State at the times and places of choosing members of the Legislature, a Secretary of State, Auditor, Treasurer, and Superintendent of Public Instruction, who shall have attained the age of twenty-five years respectively, shall be citizens of the United States, and shall have the qualification of State electors. They shall severally hold their offices at the seat of government for the term of four (4) years and until their successors are

elected and duly qualified, but no person shall be eligible for the
office of Treasurer for four (4) years after the expiration of the
term for which he was elected. The Legislature may provide
for such other State officers as are deemed necessary.

ARTICLE VII.

EDUCATION.

PUBLIC INSTRUCTION.

Sec. 1. The Legislature shall provide for the establishment and maintenance of a complete and uniform system of
public instruction, embracing free elementary schools of every
needed kind and grade, a university with such technical and
professional departments as the public good may require and
the means of the State allow, and such other institutions as may
be necessary.

PERPETUAL FUNDS FOR SCHOOLS DESIGNATED.

Sec. 2. The following are declared to be perpetual funds
for school purposes, of which the annual income only can be
appropriated, to-wit: Such percentum as has been or may hereafter be granted by Congress on the sale of lands in this State;
all moneys arising from the sale or lease of Sections No. 16 and
36 in each township in the State, and the lands selected or that
may be selected in lieu thereof; the proceeds of all lands that
have been or may hereafter be granted to this State, where, by
the terms and conditions of the grant, the same are not to be
otherwise appropriated; the net proceeds of lands and other
property and effects that may come to the State by escheat or
forfeiture, or from unclaimed dividends or distributive shares
of the estates of deceased persons; all moneys, stocks, bonds,
lands and other property now belonging to the common school
fund.

OTHER REVENUE.

Sec. 3. To the sources of revenue above mentioned shall
be added all other grants, gifts and devises that have been or
may hereafter be made to this State and not otherwise appropriated by the terms of the grant, gift or devise.

SCHOOL MONEY, RESTRICTION ON USE.

Sec. 4. All moneys, stocks, bonds, lands and other property belonging to a county school fund, except such moneys and

property as may be provided by law for current use in aid of public schools, shall belong to and be securely invested and sacredly preserved in the several counties as a county public school fund, the income of which shall be appropriated exclusively to the use and support of free public schools in the several counties of the State.

FINES GO TO SCHOOL FUND.

Sec. 5. All fines and penalties under general laws of the State shall belong to the public school fund of the respective counties and be paid over to the custodians of such funds for the current support of the public schools therein.

SCHOOL FUNDS, RESTRICTION ON INVESTMENT.

Sec. 6. All funds belonging to the State for public school purposes, the interest and income of which only are to be used, shall be deemed trust funds in the care of the State, which shall keep them for the exclusive benefit of the public schools, and shall make good any losses that may in any manner occur, so that the same shall remain forever inviolate and undiminished. None of such funds shall ever be invested or loaned except on the bonds issued by school districts, or registered county bonds of the State, or State securities of this State, or of the United States.

APPLICATION OF INCOME.

Sec. 7. The income arising from the funds mentioned in the preceding section, together with all the rents of the unsold school lands and such other means as the Legislature may provide, shall be exclusively applied to the support of free schools in every county in the State.

DISTRIBUTION OF INCOME.

Sec. 8. Provision shall be made by general law for the equitable distribution of such income among the several counties according to the number of children of school age in each; which several counties shall in like manner distribute the proportion of said fund by them received respectively to the several school districts embraced therein. But no appropriation shall be made from said fund to any district for the year in which a school has not been maintained for at least three months; nor shall any portion of any public school fund ever be used to support or assist any private school, or any school, academy, seminary, college or other institution of learning controlled by any

church or sectarian organization or religious denomination
whatsoever.

TAXATION FOR SCHOOLS.

Sec. 9.   The Legislature shall make such further provision
by taxation or otherwise, as with the income arising from the
general school fund will create and maintain a thorough and
efficient system of public schools, adequate to the proper instruction of all the youth of the State, between the ages of six
and twenty-one years, free of charge; and in view of such provision so made, the Legislature shall require that every child
of sufficient physical and mental ability shall attend a public
school during the period between six and eighteen years for a
time equivalent to three years, unless educated by other
means.

NO DISCRIMINATION AS TO PUPILS.

Sec. 10.   In none of the public schools so established and
maintained shall distinction or discrimination be made on account of sex, race or color.

TEXT BOOKS.

Sec. 11.   Neither the Legislature nor the Superintendent
of Public Instruction shall have power to prescribe text books
to be used in the public schools.

SECTARIAN INSTRUCTION PROHIBITED.

Sec. 12.   No sectarian instruction, qualifications or tests
shall be imparted, exacted, applied or in any manner tolerated
in schools of any grade or character controlled by the State,
nor shall attendance be required at any religious service therein, nor shall any sectarian tenets or doctrines be taught or
favored in any public school or institution that may be established under the constitution.

BOARD OF LAND COMMISSIONERS.   (See note following this sec-
tion.)

Sec. 13.   The Governor, Secretary of State, State Treasurer and Superintendent of Public Instruction shall constitute
the Board of Land Commissioners, which, under direction of
the Legislature, as limited by this Constitution, shall have direction, control, leasing and disposal of the lands of the State
granted, or which may be hereafter granted for the support
and benefit of public schools, subject to the further limitations

that the sale of all lands shall be at public auction, after such
delay (not less than the time fixed by Congress) in portions at
proper intervals of time, and at such minimum prices (not less
than the minimum fixed by Congress) as to realize the largest
possible proceeds.

THE BOARD OF LAND COMMISSIONERS.

(Note—Relative to Board of Land Commissioners designated by the
Legislature under the foregoing Constitutional provision—The following
extract is made from laws of 1890-91, ch, 79, page 332, viz: "Section 1.
The Governor, Superintendent of Public Instruction and Secretary of
State being constituted a State Board of Land Commissioners by the
Constitution of this State, shall, as such Board, have the direction,
management and control of all lands belonging to the State, and shall
manage the same to the best interests of the State, and in accordance
with the provisions of this act and the Constitution of the State." The
same law also provides: "Sec. 47. The funds arising from the sale or
lease of its agricultural college, scientific school, normal school common
school, charitable and penal institution lands, shall be held intact for
the benefit of the funds for which said lands are granted, and the interest and rental only shall be expended for the purpose of the grant.")

SUPERVISION OF PUBLIC SCHOOLS.

Sec. 14. The general supervision of the public schools
shall be entrusted to the State Superintendent of Public Instruction, whose powers and duties shall be prescribed by law.

THE UNIVERSITY.

STATE UNIVERSITY—UNIVERSITY LANDS—LEASES.

Sec. 15. The establishment of the University of Wyoming
is hereby confirmed, and the said institution, with its several
departments, is hereby declared to be the University of the
State of Wyoming. All lands which have been heretofore
granted, or which may be granted hereafter by Congress unto
the University, as such, or in aid of the instruction to be given
in any of its departments, with all other grants, donations or
devises for said University, and be exclusively used for the purposes for which they were granted, donated or devised. The
said lands may be leased on terms approved by the Land Commissioners, but may not be sold on terms not approved by Congress.

OPEN TO ALL—SUPPORT OF.

Sec. 16. The University shall be equally open to students
of both sexes, irrespective of race or color; and, in order that

the instruction furnished may be as nearly free as possible, any amount in addition to the income from its grants of lands and other sources above mentioned, necessary to its support and maintenance in a condition of full efficiency, shall be raised by taxation or otherwise under provisions of the Legislature.

TRUSTEES.

Sec. 17.   The Legislature shall provide by law for the management of the University, its lands and other property by a Board of Trustees, consisting of not less than seven members, to be appointed by the Governor, by and with the advice and consent of the Senate, and the President of the University, and the Superintendent of Public Instruction, as members ex-officio, as such having the right to speak, but not to vote.   The duties and powers of the Trustees shall be prescribed by law.

(For further information concerning the State University, catalogues may be obtained gratuitously, postage paid, upon application to the Secretary of the Board or President of the University at Laramie, Wyoming.)

PERMANENT LOCATION OF THE CAPITAL, STATE UNIVERSITY, ETC., TO BE SUBMITTED.

Sec. 23.   The Legislature shall have no power to change or locate the seat of government, the State University, Insane asylum, or State Penitentiary, but may, after the expiration of ten (10) years after the adoption of this Constitution, provide by law for submitting the question of the permanent locations thereof, respectively, to the qualified electors of the State, at some general election, and a majority of all votes upon said question cast at said election, shall be necessary to determine the location thereof; but for said period of ten (10) years, and until the same are respectively and permanently located, as herein provided, the location of the seat of government and said institutions shall be as follows:

The seat of government shall be located at the City of Cheyenne, in the County of Laramie; the State University shall be located at the City of Laramie, in the County of Albany; the Insane Asylum shall be located at the Town of Evanston, in the County of Uinta; the Penitentiary shall be located at the City of Rawlins, in the County of Carbon; but the Legislature may provide by law that said Penitentiary may be converted to other public uses.   The Legislature shall not locate any other public institutions except under general laws and by vote of the people.

ARTICLE XV.

TAXATION AND REVENUE.

*   *   *   *   *

LIMITATION OF STATE LEVY.

Sec. 4. For State revenue, there shall be levied annually a tax not to exceed four mills on the dollar of the assessed valuation of the property in the State, except for the support of State educational and charitable institutions, the payment of the State debt and the interest thereon.

COUNTY LEVY LIMITED—POLL TAX.

Sec. 5. For county revenue, there shall be levied annually a tax not to exceed twelve mills on the dollar for all purposes, including general school tax, exclusive of State revenues, except for the payment of its public debt and the interest thereon. An additional tax of two dollars for each person between the ages of twenty-one and fifty years, inclusive, shall be annually levied for county school purposes.

*   *   *   *   *

PUBLIC MONEY NOT TO BE A SOURCE OF PROFIT TO OFFICER.

Sec. 8. The making of profit, directly or indirectly, out of State, county, city, town or school district money or other pubilc fund, or using the same for any purpose not authorized by law, by any public officer, shall be deemed a felony, and shall be punished as provided by law.

*   *   *   *   *

EXEMPTION FROM TAXATION.

Sec. 12. The property of the United States, the State, counties, cities, towns, school districts, municipal corporations and public libraries, lots with the buildings thereon used exclusively for religious worship, church parsonages, public cemeteries, shall be exempt from taxation, and such other property as the Legislature may by general law provide.

*   *   *   *   *

CONSTITUTION.

ARTICLE XVI.

PUBLIC INDEBTEDNESS.

CERTAIN DONATIONS PROHIBITED—INTERNAL IMPROVE-MENT.

Sec. 6. Neither the State, nor any county, city, township, town, school district, or any other political sub-division, shall loan or give its credit, or make donations to or in aid of any individual, association or incorporation, except for necessary support of the poor, nor subscribe to or become the owner of the capital stock of any association or corporation. The State shall not engage in any work of internal improvement unless authorized by a two-thirds vote of the people.

*   *   *   *   *

CERTIFICATE AS TO DEBT LIMIT REQUIRED.

Sec. 8. No bond or evidence of indebtedness of the State shall be valid unless the same shall have endorsed thereon a certificate signed by the Auditor and Secretary of State that the bond or evidence of debt is issued pursuant to law and is within the debt limit. No bond or evidence of debt of any county, or bond of any township or other political sub-division, shall be valid unless the same shall have been endorsed thereon a certificate signed by the county auditor or other officer authorized by law to sign such certificate, stating that said bond or evidence of debt is issued pursuant to law and is within the debt limit.

ARTICLE XVIII.

PUBLIC LANDS AND DONATIONS.

ACCEPTANCE OF GRANTS BY THE UNITED STATES.

Section 1. The State of Wyoming hereby agrees to accept the grants of lands heretofore made, or that may hereafter made by the United States to the State, for educational purposes, for public buildings and institutions, and for other objects, and donations of money with the conditions and limitations that may be imposed by the act or acts of Congress, making such grants or donations, such lands shall be disposed of only at public auction to the highest responsible bidder, after-having been duly appraised by the Land Commissioners, at not less than three-fourths of the appraised value thereof, and for not less than $10 per acre; Provided, That in case of actual and bona fide settlement and improvement thereon at the time of the aoption of this Constitution, such actual settlers have the preference right ro purchase the land whereon he may have settled, not exceeding 160 acres, at a sum not less than the appraised value thereof, and in making such appraisement the value of improvements shall not be taken into consideration. If, at any time hereafter, the United States shall grant any arid lands in the State to the State, on the condition that the State reclaim and dispose of them to actual settlers, the Legislature shall be authorized to accept such arid lands on such conditions, or other conditions, if the same are practicable and reasonable.

APPLICATION OF PROCEEDS.

Sec. 2. The proceeds from the sale and rental of all lands and other property donated, granted or received, or that may hereafter be donated, granted or received from the United States or any other source, shall be inviolately appropriated and applied to the specific purposes specified in the original grant or gifts.

STATE BOARD OF LAND COMMISSIONERS.

Sec. 3. The Governor, Superintendent of Public Instruction and Secretary of State shall constitute a Board of Land Commissioners who, under such regulations as may be provided by law, shall have the direction, control, disposition and care of all lands that have been heretofore or may hereafter be granted to the State.

LAWS TO BE PASSED FOR SALE AND LEASE OF LAND—CARE OF FUNDS.

Sec. 4. The Legislature shall enact the necessary laws for the sale, disposal, leasing or care of all lands that have been or may hereafter be granted to the State, and shall, at the earliest practicable period, provide by law for the location and selection of all lands that have been or may hereafter be granted by Congress to the State, and shall pass laws for the suitable keeping, transfer and disbursement of the land grant funds, and shall require of all officers charged with the same or the safe keeping thereof to give ample bonds for all moneys and funds received by them.

LAWS GRANTING PRIVILEGES PROHIBITED.

Sec. 5. Except a preference right to buy, as in this Constitution otherwise provided, no law shall ever be passed by the Legislature granting any privileges to persons who may have settled upon any of the school lands granted to the State subsequent to the survey thereof by the general Government, by which the amount to be derived by the sale or other disposition of such lands, shall be diminished directly or indirectly.

UNEXPENDED PROCEEDS.

Sec. 6. If any portion of the interest or income of the perpetual school fund be not expended during any year, said portion shall be added to and become a part of the said school fund.

(From the Revised Statutes of 1887 and subsequent laws.)

TITLE 45. SCHOOL LAWS.

CHAPTER 1.

SUPERINTENENT OF PUBLIC INSTRUCTION.

Section.
3906. General duties of Superintendent.
3907. Disposition of donated books, maps, etc.
3908. Superintendent may grant teachers certificates.

GENERAL DUTIES OF SUPERINTENDENT.

Sec. 3906. The duties of Superintendent shall be as follows: He shall file all papers, reports and public documents transmitted to him by the school officers of the several counties, each year, separately, and hold the same in readiness to be exhibited to the Governor, or to any committees of either house of the Legislative Assembly; and shall keep a fair record of all matter pertaining to the business of his office. He shall have a general supervision of all the district schools of the State, and shall see that the school system is, as early as practicable, put in uniform operation. He shall prepare and have printed suitable forms for all reports required by this title, and shall transmit the same, with such instructions in reference to the course of studies as he may judge advisable, to the several officers entrusted with their management and care. He shall make all further rules and regulations that may be necessary to carry the law into full effect, according to its spirit and intent, which shall have the same force and effect as though contained herein. He shall make a report to the Legislative Assembly on the first day of each regular session thereof, exhibiting the condition of the public schools, and such other matters relating to the affairs of his office as he may think proper to communicate. (C. L. 1876, ch. 103, p. 526, sec. 2.)

Note—The foregoing section (No. 3906) is amended by sec. 1, ch. 5, law of 1890, amending sections 4 and 5 of an act providing for reports of Territorial officers and boards of public institutions, and for other purposes, approved March 8th, 1888, as follows:

(EXTRACT.)

*   *   *   *   *

REPORTS.

"Sec. 4.   Biennially, on or before the first day of November immediately preceding the meeting of the Legislative Assembly, each and every Territorial officer (except those mentioned in the last preceding section) and each and every commission or board of a Territorial institution, shall report in writing to the Governor of the Territory, the condition of his department or its institution, as required by law, covering the period since the last report and up to and including the thirtieth day of September. The reports thus required shall be made in triplicate, one copy to be filed in the office of the Governor, one copy for the use of the Council and one for the use of the House of Representatives."   *   *   *   *
Approved February 13, 1890.

DISPOSITION OF DONATED BOOKS, MAPS, ETC.

Sec. 3907.   One copy of all books, maps, charts or school apparatus, which may be received by the Superintendent of Public Instruction from publishers, inventors or manufacturers, shall be placed by him in the public library of this Territory. (C. L. 1876, ch. 103, p. 526, sec. 3.)

SUPERINTENDENT MAY GRANT TEACHERS' CERTIFICATES.

Sec. 3908.   The Superintendent of Public Instruction shall also have power to grant certificates of qualification to teachers of proper learning and ability, to teach in any public school in the Territory, and to regulate the grade of county certificates. (C. L. 1876, ch. 103, sec. 4.)

Note—Sections 3909, 3910, 3911, 3912 and 3913 repealed, laws of 1888, page 165.

CHAPTER 2.

DUTIES OF COUNTY SUPERINTENDENT.

ENUMERATION OF DUTIES AND POWERS.

Sec. 3914, (as amended by laws of 1888, ch. 67, pages 141 and 142). The duties of the County Superintendent of Schols shall be as follows: He shall, on the first Monday of October of each year, transmit to the Superintendent of Public Instruction a report containing an abstract of the several particulars set forth in the reports of the district clerks, together with a statement of the financial affairs of his office and such suggestions as he may think proper relative to the schools of his county. He shall distribute to the districts within his county such blank forms, circulars and other communications as may be transmitted to him for that purpose by the Superintendent of Public Instruction. On the first Monday in December annually he shall appertion the county school tax and all money in the county treasury beloning to the county school fund in the following manner: Each school district in his county shall be apportioned the sum of one hundred and fifty dollars for the payment of teachers in such district, and all moneys remaining after such apportionment shall be apportioned to each district pro rata, according to the number of pupils in attendance in the schools of said district reported to him by the several district clerks; but no district shall be entitled to the amount of one hundred and fifty dollars for the payment of teachers beside the pro rata apportionment as provided in this section when there are less than eight scholars of school age in said district; and he shall record a statement thereof in his office, and he shall also notify the county treasurer of such apportionment. He shall immediately draw an order on the county treasurer in favor of the treasurer of each district for the amount of its proportion, and transmit the same to the treasurer of the district: Provided, Such district treasurer shall have given his official bond, which draft the county treasurer shall pay to the district treasurer on presentation of the draft properly endorsed. Should no apportionment of the school funds of the county be made on the first Monday in December, as required in this section, he may make an apportionment as soon thereafter as practicable, in the same manner as hereinbefore provided. He

2

may also make a supplementary apportionment of the money
in the county school fund at any time after the first Monday in
December prior to the first of the following June, and such
supplementary apportionment shall be pro rata, according to
the number of pupils in attendance in any and all schools in
each district as reported to him by the several district clerks
in their last annual reports. He shall divide the settled parts
of the county into school districts, and may alter and change
the boundaries of districts thus formed from time to time as the
convenience of the inhabitants of the aforesaid districts may
require, and shall proceed to make such change at any time
when petitioned by two-thirds of the legal voters of any district.
He shall examine every person offering himself or herself as
teacher of public schools, and if in his opinion such person is
qualified to teach a public school, shall give him or her a certificate authorizing him or her to teach a public school in his
county for one year. Whenever practicable, the examinations
of teachers shall be competitive, and the certificate shall be
granted according to the qualifications of the applicant. He
shall have the general superintendence of the schools in his
county, and shall visit each school at least once each term, and
shall have power to dismiss all teachers he may find to be incompetent. (Approved March 9, 1888.)

FAILURE TO MAKE REPORT—PENALTY.

Sec. 3915. Should he fail to make his reports, as required
in the foregoing section, he shall forfeit the sum of one hundred
dollars, and suit shall be brought on his official bond for the
collection of the same. with damages, by the Prosecuting Attorney. (C. L. 1876, ch. 103, sec. 8.)

MAY GRANT TEACHERS' CERTIFICATES FOR TWO YEARS—RENEWALS.

Sec. 3916. The County Superintendent of any county in
the Territory may, if in his opinion the interest of the schools
will be as well served, grant a certificate to any person of requisite ability and qualification, for two years or during his term
of office, or may renew a certificate previously given to such
person without a re-examination. (S. L. 1882, ch. 101, sec. 3.)

SUPERVISORY AND APPELLATE AUTHORITY.

Sec. 3917. He shall see that the annual reports of the
clerks of the several school districts in his county are made cor-
rectly and in due time, and shall hear and determine all appeals

from the decision of the district boards. (C. L. 1876, ch. 103, sec. 9.)

CHAPTER 3.

SCHOOL DISTRICTS—ORGANIZATION AND POWERS.

NOTICE OF FORMATION OF NEW DISTRICT.

Sec. 3918. Whenever a school district shall be formed in any county, the County Superintendent of Schools in such county shall, within fifteen days thereafter, prepare a notice of the formation of such district, describing its boundaries and stating the number thereof, and appointing a time and place for the district meeting. He shall cause the notice, thus prepared, to be posted in at least five public places in the district, at least ten days before the time appointed for such meeting; and when a joint district is derived from portions of two or more counties, the County Superintendent of each county, from which any portion of the new district is taken, shall unite in giving the customary notices, and the new district shall be numbered by the superintendent of the county having the highest number of districts. (C. L. 1876, ch. 103, sec. 10.)

APPEAL FROM SUPERINTENDENT ON FORMATION OF NEW DISTRICT.

Sec. 3919. A majority of the voters in any school district, being dissatisfied with the formation of any school district, shall have the right to appeal from the Superintendent to the Board of County Commissioners, and from the Board of County Commissioners to the Superintendent of Public Instruction. (C. L. 1876, ch. 103, sec. 11.)

QUALIFICATIONS OF ELECTORS.

Sec. 3920. All citizens over the age of twenty-one years, who have resided for thirty days within such district, and who are liable to pay school tax therein, or in the county and none others, shall be deemed qualified electors at school meetings held within such district; Provided, That after the first year of the organization of any school district, no person shall be deemed a qualified elector at any such meetings, who, being liable to pay a school tax therein, or in the county in the year preceding, hath failed to pay the same; Provided further, That the qualifications of a voter at regular school district elections for District Trustees shall be as provided in section 3932. (C. L. 1876, ch. 103, sec. 13. S. L. 1886, ch. 93, sec. 2.)

MEETING TO ELECT TRUSTEES.

Sec. 3921, (as amended and re-enacted by laws of 1890, chap. 77, pages 153 and 154). "The qualified electors of a schol district, when assembled in accordance with the notice required in Section 3918, shall organize by appointing a chairman and secretary, who shall act as judges of the election. They shall then by ballot elect three trustees possessing the qualifications of electors of said district, and the name of each elector shall be recorded by the secretary, and they shall hold their office until the next succeeding annual district election, and until their successors are elected and qualified. The said Trustees shall constitute a Board of Directors for the district and shall, as soon as they are qualified, choose from their number a Director, Treasurer and Clerk of the district." (Approved March 11, 1890.)

ELECTION OF TRUSTEES WHERE NUMBER INCREASED TO SIX.

Sec. 3922. In all school districts in this Territory containing a population of two thousand or more, and in which the number of Trustees has been increased to six as provided by law, at each annual election there shall be elected two Trustees who shall hold office until the third annual election after the the time of their election. (S. L. 1879, ch. 63, secs. 1 and 2.)

SCHOOL DISTRICT SEAL.

Sec. 3923. It shall be the duty of every Board of School Directors so increased to six members, to provide at the expense of their district, and for said district, a seal, upon which shall be engraved the words, "School District No. ———, ——— Co., Wyo. Ter.," stating the number of the district and the county in which it is situated. The seal shall be in possession of the Clerk of the district. It shall be affixed to all communications or notices required by law to be sent or published by such School Board, and to all warrants drawn upon the Treasurer of the district. (S. L. 1879, ch. 63, sec.4.)

OATH OF DIRECTORS.

Sec. 3924, (as amended and re-enacted by laws of 1890, ch. 77, page154). "All Directors of the Board shall, within ten days after their election, appear before some justice of the peace or other person qualified to administer oaths, and take an oath for the faithful performance of their duties and in accordance with law, and shall, without delay, transmit a copy of said oath in writing to the County Superintendent of Schools." (Approved March 14, 1890.)

SCHOOL DISTRICT TO BE BODY CORPORATE, ETC.

Sec. 3925. Each school district formed under the provisions of this title, is hereby declared to be a body corporate by the name and style of School District No. ———, in the County of ———, and Territory of Wyoming; and in that name it may hold property, and be a party to suits and contracts. (C. L. 1876, ch. 103, sec. 15.)

REGULAR MEETINGS OF DISTRICT.

Sec. 3926. The regular meeting of each school district shall be held on the first Monday of May of each year. And, when present, the Director and Clerk shall preside as chairman and secretary of such meeting. (C. L. 1876, ch. 103, sec. 16.)

POWERS OF DISTRICT MEETING.

Sec. 5927, (as amended, sub-divisions five and eight, by laws of 1888, pag 163, and laws of 1890, page 154). The qualified electors of the district, when assembled, shall have power:

First—To appoint a chairman and secretary, in the absence of the regular officers;

Second—To adjourn from time to time, as occasion may require;

Third—To determine the number of schools which shall be established in the district, and the length of time each shall be taught;

Fourth—To fix the site of each school house, taking into consideration, in doing so, the wants and necessities of the people of each portion of the district;

Fifth—"To vote such sum of money as the meeting shall deem sufficient for any of the following purposes: To supply any deficiency in the fund for the payment of teachers; to purchase or lease a suitable site for a school house, or school houses; to build, rent or purchase a school house, or school houses; and keep in repair and furnish the same with the necessary fuel and appendages; for procuring libraries for the schools, books and stationery for the use of the Board and district meetings; for purchasing books for indigent scholars and to defray all other contingent expenses of the district; Provided, That the sum of money so voted shall not exceed ten mills on the dollar of all taxable property in each school district; Provided further, That the tax to be levied and collected as authorized by this section, shall not exceed five mills on the dollar of the assessed valuation of the taxable property in any one year in all school districts having a total valuation of property exceeding three millions of dollars, or a valuation thereof of less than two hundred thousand dollars." (Approved March 9, 1888.)

Sixth—To direct the sale or other disposition to be made of any school house, or the site thereof, and of such other property, real or personal, as may belong to the district, and to direct the manner in which the proceeds arising therefrom shall be applied;

Seventh—To vote a sum not exceeding one hundred dollars in any one year, to procure a district library, consisting of such books as they may direct any person to procure;

Eighth—"To delegate any and all powers specified in the foregoing sub-divisions to the District Board; Provided, always, That the District Board shall not have power to vote or raise money as provided in sub-division fifth as amended and re enacted in Chapter 1, Section 12, page 163, Session Laws of the Territory of Wyoming, A. D. 1888." (Approved March 14, 1890.)

Ninth—To transact generally such business as may tend to promote the cause of education in accordance with the provisions of this chapter. (C. L. 1876, ch. 103, sec. 17. S. L. 1886, ch. 75, sec. 1.)

OBJECTS IN VOTING MONEY TO BE DESIGNATED.

Sec. 3928. In voting money, the district meetings shall designate the respective objects for which the same is raised, and the amount to be raised for each object, and the aggregate amount shall be assessed and collected, as provided in this title. (C. L. 1876, ch. 103, sec. 18.)

MEETING MAY ADOPT RULES OF ORDER.

Sec. 3929. They may adopt rules of order, not incompatible with the provisions of this chapter and the instructions of the Superintendent of Public Instruction, for the government of district meetings, and may alter and change the same from time to time as occasion may require, and may prescribe the manner of taking the sense of the meeting upon any question; Provided, That the last specification shall not apply to the election of officers. (C. L. 1876, ch. 103, sec. 19.)

TRANSFER OF SCHOOL FUNDS.

Sec. 3930. In all cases where there are moneys belonging to the school house fund, remaining in the hands of the district Treasurer of any school district, and the Board of Directors thereof are satisfied that such moneys are not required to build a school house, or school houses, in said district, or repair or furnish the same, such moneys may be transferred and accredited to the teachers' fund, and applied to the payment of teachers. And the Board may also in like manner transfer a surplus of the teachers' fund to the fund for building school houses when required. (C. L. 1876, ch. 103, sec. 20.)

MANNER OF CONDUCTING ELECTIONS OF TRUSTEES.

Sec. 3931, (as amended and re-enacted by laws of 1888, ch. 73, pages 165 and 166). "At the regular district meeting of school districts in each year, at the time now provided by law for the election of Trustees, such district meeting shall be opened by proclamation of the Trustees, at the hour named in the published or posted notices for the meeting. And the order of business at such meeting shall be:

ORDER OF BUSINESS OF DISTRICT MEETING.

1. Reading and consideration of the report of the Clerk and Treasurer.

3. Voting of money to be raised by special tax.

5. Election of Trustee or Trustees.

4. Miscellaneous business."

(Approved March 9, 1888.)

QUALIFICATIONS OF ELECTORS IN VOTING FOR TRUSTEES.

Sec. 3932. Every legal voter in this Territory, who shall have been a bona fide resident of said district for three months next preceding any such district election, and who has paid a poll tax for the support of common schools within the Territory for the preceding year, shall be entitled and qualified to vote at such school district election for District Trustees. (S. L. 1886, ch. 93, sec. 2.)

ANNUAL ELECTION OF DISTRICT OFFICERS.

Sec. 3933, (as amended and re-enacted, laws of 1890, ch. 77, page 154). "Except as otherwise provided by law, there shall be elected in each organized school district at the regular annual district meeting on the first Monday in May of each year, one Trustee, who shall hold his office for three years and until his successor is duly elected and qualified. If for any cause the annual election should not be held at the regular annual meeting, a special meeting may be held for that purpose if so specified in the notice for said special meeting. The Trustees together shall constitute a Board of Directors for the district, and shall, immediately after they are qualified, elect one of their number a Director, Treasurer and Clerk of the district. At the first regular annual election after a school district is organized there shall be three Trustees elected, one to hold his office for the term of three years, and one to hold his office for the term of two years, and one for the term of one year, and until their successors are elected and qualified, and thereafter at each annual meeting there shall be one Trustee elected as aforesaid for the term of three years as successor to the outgoing member of the Board, and all of said Trustees herein mentioned shall possess the qualifications of an elector in said district and shall be elected by ballot, and the name of each elector voting for Trustee shall be recorded by the secretary of the meeting, and such record shall be filed with the District Clerk."

(Approved March 14, 1890.)

DIRECTORS SHALL QUALIFY.

Sec. 3934.   Said Directors shall qualify in the manner prescribed for Directors elected upon the formation of a new school
district; and in case they refuse or neglect so to do, they shall
be subject to the same penalty. (C. L. 1876, ch. 103, sec. 22.)

MEETINGS OF BOARDS.

Sec. 3935.   The Board of Directors may hold such regular
special or adjourned meetings as they may from time to time
determine. (C. L. 1876, ch. 103, sec 23.)

POWERS AND DUTIES OF DISTRICT BOARD.

Sec. 3936.   The District Board shall make all contracts,
purchases, payments and sales necessary to carry out every
vote of the district, for procuring any site for a school house,
renting, repairing or furnishing the same, and disposing thereof,
or for keeping a school therein, and performing such other
duties as may be delegated to them by the district meeting.
(C. L. 1876, ch. sec. 14.)

AUTHORITY OF BOARD TO ADMIT OR REMOVE SCHOLARS.

Sec. 3937.   The District Board shall have power to admit
scholars from adjoining districts, and remove scholars for dis-
orderly conduct; and when scholars are admitted from other
districts the District Board may in their discretion, require a
tuition fee from such scholars. (C. L. 1876, ch. 103, sec. 25.)

WHEN BOARD SHALL ADVERTISE FOR BIDS BEFORE CON-
    TRACTING.

Sec. 3938.   Whenever any school house is to be built or
any repairs, addition or improvement costing more than two
hundred dollars made to any school house or district property,
the Board of Directors of the district shall advertise for bids
for such work, and in all cases contract the same to the lowest
responsible bidder. (S. L. 1886, ch. 93, sec. 8.)

SETTLEMENT   WITH   TREASURERS—REPORT   TO   DISTRICT
    MEETING.

Sec. 3939.   They shall, from time to time, examine the
books and accounts of the Treasurer, and make settlement with
him, and shall, at each regular meeting of the district, present
to the same a full statement of the receipts and expenditures
of the district, and such other matters as may be deemed important. (C. L. 1876, ch. 103, sec. 28.)

VISITING COMMITTEE.

Sec. 3910. They shall appoint a committee from their own body to visit the respective schools of the district monthly, and to aid the teachers in establishing and enforcing rules for the government of schools, and see that the teachers keep a correct list of the pupils, the time which they attend school, the branches of learning which each is studying, and such other matters as may, in the opinion of the Board, tend to promote the welfare of the school. (C. L. 1876, ch. 103, sec. 29.)

AUDITING AND PAYING DEMANDS.

Sec. 3941. They shall audit and allow all just claims against the district, and the Directors shall draw an order for all demands thus audited, on the district Treasurer. (C. L. 1876, ch. 103, sec. 30.)

SPECIAL DISTRICT MEETING—REQUISITES OF NOTICE.

Sec. 3942. They shall, upon the written request of five legal voters of the district, or, whenever they deem it expedient, call special meetings thereof; but in all such cases, the notice of such meeting shall clearly state the precise object for which it is called, and the time and place at which it is to be held. (C. L. 1876, ch. 103, sec. 31.)

For notice of district meetings see section 3956.

TERM OF EXISTING APPOINTEES TO FILL VACANCIES.

Sec. 3943. In case a vacancy in any district School Board, caused by the resignation, death or otherwise of any one of its members, is or has been filled by appointment, said appointee may legally hold said office until the next annual school election following said appointment, but no longer, and at the annual election said vacancy shall be filled in the same way and manner as authorized by law for the annual election of School Trustees. (S. L. 1886, ch. 93, sec. 6.)

VACANCY IN BOARD HOW FILLED.

Sec. 3944. When a vacancy occurs in any School Board by the resignation, death or otherwise of any of its members, three months or more before the following annual school election, said vacancy cannot be filled by appointment, but a special election must be called in the way provided by law for the purpose of filling such vacancy; but if such vacancy occurs less than three months before the next annual school election, such vacancy shall be filled by appointment by the Board. (S. L. 1886, ch. 93, sec. 7.   C. L. 1876, ch. 103, sec. 32.)

BOND OF DISRICT TREASURER.

Sec. 3945.   The district Treasurer shall give bonds to the district in such penalty and with such sureties as the Board of the County Commissioners shall direct and approve, conditioned for the faithful application of all money which may come into his hands by virtue of his office; Provided, Said bonds shall not exceed one and one-quarter times the amount of all the school moneys handled by said Treasurer in any one year. Said penalty may be increased from time to time as the interests of the district may require. The said bond, after being approved by the Board of County Commissioners, shall be filed with the County Treasurer, and it is hereby made unlawful for the County Treasurer to pay over any sums of money out of the school fund to any district Treasurer until such bond shall have been approved and filed as herein provided, and in case of a breach in the conditions of said bond, suit shall be brought thereon by the Board of the County Commissioners of the county in which the district is situated, for the benefit of said district. (S. L. 1884, ch. 81, sec. 1.)

ESTABLISHMENT OF HIGH SCHOOLS.

Sec. 3946.   The County Superintendent and district Board of Directors may determine whether a school of a higher grade shall be established in the district, the number of teachers to be employed, and the course of instruction to be pursued therein, until the meeting of the Teachers' Institute, provided for by law, at which time the Institute shall determine the studies to be pursued in all schools of like grade in the Territory; and the Superintendent of Public Instruction shall have the power to carry into effect the determination of the Institute as is provided in other cases; and the Board may erect, for the purpose, one or more permanent school houses, and shall cause such classification of the pupils as they may deem necessary, but in selecting the site for such school house, or school houses, the permanent interest and future welfare of the people of the entire district shall be consulted. (C. L. 1876, ch. 103, sec. 33.)

SEPARATE SCHOOL FOR COLORED CHILDREN.

Sec. 3947.   Where there are fifteen or more colored children within any school district, the Board of Directors thereof, with the approval of County Superintendent of Schools, may provide a separate school for the instruction of such colored children. (C. L. 1876, ch. 103, sec. 34.)

EMPLOYMENT AND PAYMENT OF TEACHERS.

Sec. 3948. The district Board shall employ all teachers necessary for the schools of the district, and pay them by draft on the Treasurer. (C. L. 1876, ch, 103, sec. 35.)

SCHOOL AGE—COMPULSORY EDUCATION.

Sec. 3949. The district schools established under the provisions of this title shall at all times be equally free and accessible to all children resident therein, over six and under the age of twenty-one years, subject to such regulations as the district Board in each district may prescribe. And it shall be the duty of all parents and guardians or other persons having the control of children between the ages above mentioned, to send such children to some school, at least three months in each and every year, except in case of invalids, and others to whom the school room would be injurious. In such cases, the district Board shall, upon receipt of a physician's certificate, excuse such children; and the district Board may, in its discretion, excuse children from attendance when a compliance with this title would work great hardship. In all such cases the Clerk of the Board shall state the reason for excuse, and the name of the child or person excused, and the length of time for which excused, at large in the minutes of the proceedings of the Board; Provided, That in all cases the applicant may appeal from the decision of the Board to the County Superintendent, whose decision shall be final. (C. L. 1876, ch. 103, sec. 36.)

LIABILITY OF PARENTS AND GUARDIANS—AUTHORITY OF POLICE OFFICERS.

Sec. 3950. Any parent or guardian, or other person, having children in their charge between the ages of seven and sixteen years, who shall neglect or refuse to comply with the provisions of this chapter, shall, on conviction, be punished by a fine not exceeding twenty-five dollars, for each and every offense, and it shall be the duty of all sheriffs, constables or police officers, at all times, whenever it comes to their knowledge that any child is living idly and loitering about the streets or thoroughfares and spending its time in an idle and dissolute manner, to notify some member of the School Board of the district in which such child is living whose duty it shall be to immediately make all the proper inquiries to ascertain the

reasons for the non-attendance of said child in some school of
the county in which such child may be found by said Board;
if any such child or ward is wilfully violating the conditions
of this law, it shall become the duty of the County Superintendent of Schools, on written notice from the Board, to make a
complaint before some justice of the peace against the parent
or guardian of said child or ward, or to make complaint
against such child or ward, as provided in cases of vagrancy,
under the laws of this Territory. (C. L. 1876, ch. 103, sec. 37.
S. L. 1877, pp. 116 and 117, sec. 1.)

CHAPTER 4.

DISTRICT OFFICERS AND THEIR DUTIES.

DIRECTOR TO PRESIDE AT MEETINGS AND COUNTERSIGN
ORDERS.

Sec. 3951. The Director, when present, shall preside at
all meetings of the Board of the district, and countersign all
orders on the treasury for the payment of money. (C. L. 1876,
ch. 103, sec. 38.)

HOW DRAFTS AND ORDERS DRAWN.

Sec. 3952. All drafts and orders drawn on the district
Treasurer, as required in the foregoing section, shall specify
the fund on which they are drawn, and the use for which the
money is designed, and shall be signed by the District Clerk.
(C. L. 1876, ch. 103, sec. 39.)

BY WHOM DISTRICT TO APPEAR IN ACTIONS.

Sec. 3953. The Director shall appear in behalf of his district, in all suits brought by or against the same; but when he
is individually a party, this duty shall be performed by the
Clerk. (C. L. 1876, ch. 103, sec. 40.)

DUTIES OF CLERK.

Sec. 3954, (as amended and re-enacted by laws of 1890, ch. 77, page 154). "The Clerk shall record all the proceedings of the Board and of the district meetings in books to be kept for that purpose, and report in writing to the County Superintendent of Schools the name of the Director and Treasurer immediately after they are chosen or elected, and he shall preserve copies of all reports made to the County Superintendent, and shall file all papers transmitted to him by school officers or other persons pertaining to the business of the district, and shall sign all drafts, warrants and orders drawn by him."

(Approved March 14, 1890.)

CLERKS SHALL KEEP ACCOUNTS.

Sec. 3955. He shall keep an accurate account of all the expenses incurred by the district, and shall present the same to the district Board, to be audited and paid as herein provided, out of the school fund. (C. L. 1876, ch. 103, sec. 42.)

NOTICE OF DISTRICT MEETINGS.

Sec. 3956. He shall give ten days' previous notice of all regular and special meetings of the district, herein authorized, by posting up a written notice in three different places therein; and shall furnish a copy of the same to the teachers of each school in the district, to be read once in the presence of the pupils thereof. (C. L. 1876, ch. 103, sec. 43.)

For requisites of notice of special district meeting, see sec. 3942.

ANNUAL REPORT TO COUNTY SUPERINTENDENT.

Sec. 3957. The district Clerk shall, on the first Monday of September in each year, submit a report to the County Superintendent for the year past, then ending:

First—Of the number of schools taught in such district, the number of days each scholar attended the same, and the aggregate number of days of attendance of said school respectively, as certified by the teachers of the several schools of such district;

Second—The number of schools and the branches taught in each;

Third—The number of pupils in each school, and of each sex;

Fourth—The number of teachers employed in each school, and the average compensation of each per month;

Fifth—The number of days the school has been taught, and by whom;

Sixth—The average cost of tuition for a pupil, per month, in each school;

Seventh—Books used in each school;

Eighth—The number of volumes in the library of each school;

Ninth—The aggregate amount paid teachers during the year, the source from which the same was received, and the amount of the teachers' fund in the hands of the Treasurer;

Tenth—The number of district school houses, and the cost of each;

Eleventh—The amount raised in the district by tax, for the erection of school houses, and for other purposes authorized in this title, and such other information as he may deem useful. (C. L. 1876, ch. 103, sec. 44.)

FAILURE TO MAKE REPORT—PENALTY.

.Sec. 3958. Should the Clerk fail to file his reports, as above directed, he shall forfeit the sum of twenty-five dollars, and shall be liable to make good all loss resulting to the district from such failure, suit to be brought in both cases by the Director, in the name of the district, on his official bond. (C. L. 1876, ch. 103, sec. 45.)

DUTIES OF TREASURER—PUBLICATION OF REPORT.

Sec. 3959. The Treasurer shall have the custody of all moneys belonging to the district, and shall pay out the same upon the order of the Clerk, countersigned by the Director; and shall keep an account of the receipts and expenditures thereof, in a book provided for that purpose. He shall cause to be published in some newspaper of general circulation in the county wherein such school district is situate, on the first week of July in each year, a full and true report of the receipts and disbursements of said district for the year next preceding such report. (C. L. 1876, ch. 103, sec. 46. S. L. 1884, ch. 81, sec. 2.)

TEACHERS' FUND.

Sec. 3960. The moneys for the payment of teachers shall be called the "teachers' fund" and the Treasurer shall keep distinct and separate accounts with them; and no warrant for money shall be paid by the Treasurer which does not specify the fund on which it is drawn, and the specific use to which it is to be applied. (C. L. 1876, ch. 103, sec. 47.)

SCHOOL HOUSE FUND.

Sec. 3961. The school house fund shall consist only of taxes collected in the district; and the other school moneys belonging to the district shall go to the teachers' fund, and shall be applied to no other use except to pay the wages of school teachers in the district. (C. L. 1876, ch. 103, sec. 48.)

TREASURER TO RECEIVE DISTRICT MONEY.

Sec. 3962. The Treasurer shall apply for, and receive all money apportioned to the district, by the County Superintendent, when notified of such apportionment. (C. L. 1876, ch. 103, sec. 49.)

TREASURER TO RENDER STATEMENT ON REQUEST.

Sec. 3963. He shall render a statement of the finances of the district, as shown by the records of his office, at any time when required by the district Board. C. L. 1876, ch. 103, sec. 50.)

CHAPTER 5.

SCHOOL TAX AND THE COLLECTION THEREOF.

TAX LEVY FOR SCHOOL PURPOSES.

Sec. 3964. The County Commissioners shall, at the time of levying tax for county purposes, cause to be levied a tax for the support of schools within the county, as provided by law, which shall be collected by the County Collector, at the same time and in the same manner as Territorial and county taxes are collected, with the exception that it shall be receivable in cash or warrants of the school. The County Treasurer shall, at all times hold, subject to the draft of the proper officers, all moneys belonging to teachers' or school house fund. (C. L. 1876, ch. 103, sec. 51.)

DUTY OF CLERK AND ASSESSOR AS TO DISTRICT TAXES.

Sec. 3965. Whenever a sum of money has been voted by a district, the Clerk shall, under the supervision of the Director, make out and certify, over his official signature, the amount of

money voted in his district, and on or before the fourth Monday
in May, in each year, cause the same to be filed in the office of
the Clerk of the Board of County Commissioners. The Clerk
shall also, at the same time, notify the County Assessor, in
writing, of the action of the district meeting. The County
Assessor shall, at the time of making the county assessment,
also assess the property of each district from which he has received notification as aforesaid, and return to the County Clerk,
at the time of returning the county assessment roll, a separate
roll of each district by him assessed, for which services he shall
receive five dollars per day for the time actually employed in
making such separate assessment roll, which sum shall be paid
out of the treasury of each district so assessed. (C. L. 1876, ch.
103, sec. 52. S. L. 1877, p. 115, sec. 1. S. L. 1885, ch. 97, sec. 18.)

EQUALIZATION OF ASSESSMENT AND LEVY OF TAXES.

Sec. 3966. The Board of County Commissioners of each
county shall have the power and it is made their duty to equal-
ize the assessment and valuation of the taxable property of all
the several school districts in the county which is assessable by
the County Assessor, and shall also have power to add to such
assessment any taxable property in such school district not
included in the assessments as returned by the Assessor, and
which it was his duty to assess in the same manner as is or
hereafter may be provided by law for county and Territorial
purposes, and it shall be the duty of the Board of County Commissioners when making the annual levy for taxes, to levy upon
the taxable property of each school district a tax sufficient to
raise the amount of money voted in the district for the year,
which levy shall also be made upon the assessed valuation of
railroad and telegraph property in such school district as
assessed by the Territorial Board of Equalization. And the
County Clerk, in making out the annual tax list, shall carry out
in a separate column the amount of the district school tax in
the same manner as other taxes. (S. L. 1882, ch. 91, sec. 1.)

MANNER OF COLLECTING TAXES.

Sec. 3967. The taxes and assessments of all school districts for all purposes, except as otherwise specially provided by
law, shall be collected like county taxes, and all delinquent
taxes shall be returned by the collector in the same manner as
other delinquent taxes are required by law to be returned. (C.
L. 1876, ch. 103, sec. 54.)

TO WHOM SCHOOL MONEYS ARE PAID.

Sec. 3968. The amount of tax collected by the County Collector shall be paid over to the County Treasurer like other taxes, and shall be held by said County Treasurer subject to the draft of the County Superintendent, and shall be paid over accordingly: Provided, That the money collected on the district tax rolls shall be paid by the Collector directly to the Treasurer of the proper district, and take his receipt therefor. (C. L. 1876, ch. 103, sec. 55.)

CHAPTER 6.

MISCELLANEOUS PROVISIONS.

PHYSIOLOGY AND HYGIENE SHALL BE TAUGHT.

Sec. 3969. Physiology and hygiene, which shall include in each division of the subject special reference to the effects of alcohol and narcotics upon the human system, shall be included in the branches taught in the common schools of the Territory, and shall be introduced and taught, either orally or by text book, in all departments of the public schools above the second primary grade, and in all educational institutions supported wholly or in part by the Territory. (S. L. 1886, ch. 35, sec. 1.)

FAILURE TO COMPLY WITH LAST SECTION—PENALTY.

Sec. 3970. It shall be the duty of the several County and City Superintendents of Schools in the Territory, and of the Secretary of the Board of Directors of all other educational institutions receiving aid from the Territory, to report to the Territorial Superintendent of Public Instruction any failure or neglect on the part of the Board of Trustees of any school district, or the Board of Directors of any educational institution receiving aid from the Territory, to make proper provision for the teaching of the branches mentioned in the last preceding section in any or all of the schools or other educational institutions under their charge, or over which they have jurisdiction, and such failure on the part of the above mentioned officers, so reported and satisfactorily proved, shall be deemed sufficient cause for withholding the warrant for the district appropriation of school money to which such school district or educational institution would otherwise be entitled. (S. L. 1886, ch. 35, sec. 2.)

DISCRIMINATION ON ACCOUNT OF SEX OR RELIGIOUS BELIEF PROHIBITED.

Sec. 3971, (as amended and re-enacted, ch. 21, laws 1890 and 1891, page 132). "In the employment of teachers in the public schools in this State no discrimination shall be made in the question of pay on account of sex, nor on account of the religious belief of the applicant for the position of teacher, when the persons are equally qualified, and the labor is the same."

Approved December 31, 1890.)

EXAMINATION IN PHYSIOLOGY, ETC., REQUIRED.

Sec. 3972. No certificate shall be granted hereafter to any person to teach in the schools of Wyoming, who shall not pass a satisfactory examination in physiology and hygiene, with special reference to the effects of alcoholic drinks, stimulants and narcotics upon the human system. (S. L. 1886, ch. 35, sec. 3.)

TEACHERS TO MAKE REPORTS.

Sec. 3973. It shall be the duty of the teacher of every district school, or graded school, to make out and file with the District Clerk, at the expiration of each term of the school, a full report of the whole number of scholars admitted to the school during such term, distinguishing between male and female, the names of such scholars, the number of days each scholar attended the same, the aggregate number of days attendance of said schools, the text books used, the branches taught and the number of pupils engaged in the study of each of said branches. Any teacher who shall neglect or refuse to comply with the requirements of his section, shall forfeit his or her wages for teaching such school, at the discretion of the district Board. (C. L. 1876, ch. 103, sec. 56.)

REFUSAL TO DELIVER RECORDS TO SUCCESSOR—PENALTY.

Sec. 3974. Every school district Clerk or Treasurer, who shall neglect or refuse to deliver to their successors in office, all records and books belonging severally to their offices, shall be subject to a fine not exceeding five hundred dollars. (C. L. 1876, ch. 103, sec. 57.)

EMPLOYMENT OF COUNSEL.

Sec. 3975. In all cases where suits may be instituted, by, or against any of the school officers contemplated or created by this title, to enforce any of the provisions herein contained, counsel may be employed, if necessary, by the officer instituting the suit, and the expense of the suit shall be borne by the district, county or Territory in whose name, or against whom, the same may be instituted. (C. L. 1876, ch. 103, sec. 58.)

COLLECTION AND DISPOSITION OF FINES, ETC.

Sec. 3976. All fines, penalties and forfeitures provided by this title may be recovered by action in the name of the people of the Territory of Wyoming for the use of the proper school district or county, and when they accrue, belong to the respective districts or counties in which the same may have accrued; and the Treasurer for their districts, and the County Commissioners of their counties are hereby authorized to receive and apply the proceeds of such forfeitures as the interest of the permanent fund is now, or may hereafter be, applied. (C. L. 1876, ch. 103, sec. 59.)

OFFICER FAILING TO PAY OVER MONEY—PENALTY.

Sec. 3977. Any officer or person collecting or receiving any fines, forfeitures or other moneys and refusing and failing to pay over the same as required by law, shall forfeit double the amount so withheld, and interest thereon at the rate of five per cent. per month during the time of so withholding the the same. (C. L. 1876, ch. 103, sec. 60.)

EFFECT OF CHANGE IN COUNTY BOUNDARIES ON SCHOOL DISTRICTS.

Sec. 3978. If by any act of the Territorial Legislature changing the boundary line or lines of any county or counties, or forming new counties from counties already formed, any legally organized school district is or has been separated from the county to which it then belonged, and is or has been joined to another county, the members of the School Board of such school district so separated from one county and joined to another county, shall hold their respective offices until the next annual school election following said change in county boundaries; and until such annual school election said School Board may draw the public school funds for paying teachers, or other necessary legal school expenses from the school treasury of the county to which said school district formerly belonged, and in the same way and manner as said Board would have drawn and expended said public moneys had no change in county boundaries been made. (S. L. 1886, ch. 93, sec. 5.)

(Note—Sections 3979 and 3980 repealed by laws of 1890-1891, ch. 3, page 83.)   ......

TERRITORIAL TREASURER AUTHORIZED TO RECEIVE DONATIONS FOR SCHOOLS.

Sec. 3981. Whenever the Territory of Wyoming shall be entitled to receive any moneys or funds from the United States of America, or from any other source or authority, to be expended for the benefit of the public schools of the Territory, or held or in any manner applied for their benefit, the Territorial Treasurer is hereby authorized to receive and receipt for such moneys or funds, and to make such application and use of the same as may be required by law. Should such moneys or funds be donated to the Territory, and should the act of donation require such moneys or funds to be applied or held, or used in a particular manner, they shall be so applied. (S. L. 1886, ch. 101, sec. 1.)

LIABILITY OF TREASURER FOR SCHOOL MONEY.

Sec. 3982. The Territorial Treasurer shall faithfully account for all moneys or funds received pursuant to the foregoing section, and he and his sureties upon his official bond shall be liable for any failure to so account for such moneys or funds. (S. L. 1886, ch. 101, sec. 2.)

CHAPTER 72.

SCHOOLS.

An Act to provide for the bonding of school districts and for
other purposes.

Be it enacted by the Council and House of Representatives of
the Territory of Wyoming:

CHAPTER ONE—SCHOOL DISTRICT BONDS.

AUTHORITY TO CALL ELECTION TO DETERMINE UPON ISSUE OF BONDS.

Section 1. The Board of School Trustees of any school
district may, whenever a majority thereof so decide, submit to
the electors of the district the question whether the Board
shall be authorized to issue the coupon bonds of the district to
a certain amount not to exceed three per cent of the taxable
property in said district, and bearing a certain rate of interest
not exceeding eight per cent. per annum, and payable and re-
deemable at a certain time not exceeding fifteen years, for the
purpose of building one or more school houses in said district
and providing the same with necessary furniture; Provided,
That in all school districts in the Territory wherein the electors thereof at a regular meeting have heretofore authorized the
issue of bonds for the aforesaid purposes, this act shall apply,
and such bonds shall be issued as herein provided without submitting the question of voting bonds at another election therein; Provided, further, That the amount of bonds so voted does
not exceed three per centum of the assessed valuation of the
school district.

BOND ELECTION—ISSUE OF BONDS.

Sec. 2. Such elections must be held in the manner prescribed for general or special elections in school districts, and
the ballots must contain the words "Bonds, yes," or, "Bonds,
no." If the majority of the votes at such election are "Bonds,
yes," the Board of Trustees must issue such bonds in such form

as the Board may direct; they must bear the signatures of the President of the Board and be countersigned by the Clerk of the school district, and bear the district seal and be countersigned by the County Treasurer, and the coupons attached to the bonds must be signed by said President and Clerk and said County Treasurer, and each bond so issued must be registered by the County Treasurer in a book provided for that purpose, which must show the number and amount of each bond, and the person to whom the same is issued, and the said bonds must be sold by the said School Trustees, as hereinafter provided.

SALE OF BONDS—APPLICATION OF PROCEEDS.

Sec. 3.   The School Trustees must give notice in some newspaper of general circulation, published in the capital of this Territory, and also in some newspaper published in the county in which said school district is located, for a period of not less than four weeks, to the effect that the said School Trustees will sell said bonds, briefly describing the same, and the time and place where such sale will take place; Provided, That the said bonds must not be sold for less than their par value, and the said Trustees are authorized to reject any bids, and to sell said bonds at private sale, if they deem it for the best interests of the district; and all the money arising from the sale of said bonds must be paid forthwith into the treasury of the county in which said district may be located, to the credit of said district, and the same shall be immediately available for the purpose of building or providing the school house or school houses authorized by this act.

PLEDGE OF PAYMENT.

Sec. 4.   The faith of such school district is solemnly pledged for the payment of the interest, and the redemption of the principal of all bonds which are issued under this act.

TAX LEVY TO REDEEM AND PAY INTEREST.

Sec. 5.   The Board of County Commissioners of the proper county of each district must ascertain and levy annually, the tax necessary to pay the interest as it becomes due, and a sinking fund to redeem the said bonds at their maturity; and said tax is a lien upon the property in said school district, and must be collected in the same manner as other taxes for school purposes.   Said tax shall be known as "district bond tax of school district No. ——."

REDEMPTION.

Sec. 6. When the sum in the sinking fund equals or exceeds the amount of any bond then due, the County Treasurer shall post in his office a notice that he will, within thirty days from the date of such notice, redeem the bonds then payable, giving the number thereof, and the preference must be given to the oldest issue, and if, at the expiration of the said thirty days, the holder or holders of said bonds shall fail or neglect to present the same for payment, interest thereon must ceas·; but the Treasurer shall at all times thereafter be ready to redeem the same on presentation, and when any bonds are so purchased or redeemed, the County Treasurer must cancel the same by writing across the face of each bond, in red ink, the word "cancelled," and date of such cancellation. The annual interest on all of said bonds shall be payable at the office of the Treasurer of the proper county on the first and ten succeeding days of January in each year.

PAYMENT OF INTEREST.

Sec. 7. The County Treasurer may pay out of any moneys belonging to a school district tax fund, the interest on any bonds issued under this act by such school district, when the same becomes due, upon the presentation at his office of the proper coupon, which must show the amount due and the number of the bond to which it belonged, and all coupons so paid must be reported to the School Trustees at their first regular meeting thereafter.

PREPARATION OF BONDS.

Sec. 8. The School Trustees of any district shaal cause to be printed or lithographed at the lowest rates suitable bonds, with the coupons attached, when the same become necessary, and pay therefor out of any moneys in their treasury.

PENALTY FOR MIS-APPLICATION OF FUNDS BY TRUSTEES.

Sec. 9. If any of the School Trustees fraudulently fail or refuse to pay into the proper county treasury the money arising from the sale of any bonds provided for by this act, they shall be deemed guilty of felony and upon conviction thereof, be punished by imprisonment in the Territorial Penitentiary for a term of not less than one year, nor more than ten years.

COUNTY TREASURER SHALL HAVE CUSTODY OF FUNDS—FEES.

Sec. 10. The County Treasurer of such county shall have the custody of all funds realized from the sale of said bonds, until the same are drawn out by order of the Board of Directors of said district, *and he shall be entitled to and receive one-half of one per cent. commission for safe keeping and accounting for the same; Provided, That said County Treasurer shall not be entitled to any commission on any funds turned over to his successor in office.

ADDITIONAL BOND OF COUNTY TREASURER.

Sec. 11. The Board of Trustees of said district shall require the same County Treasurer to give said district a separate bond in such sum as said Board may deem proper, with two or more sufficient sureties, conditioned for the faithful performance of the duties required of him by this act and the faithful accounting for the moneys deposited with him and realized from the sale of said bonds, as herein provided for, and such bond shall be approved by said Board and shall be and remain in the custody of said Board of Trustees.

Sec. 12. (Amending sub-division 5, section 3927, Revised Statutes, see page 22 of this compilation.)

Chapter 2—Misdemeanors Concerning Schools.

THE OFFENSES DEFINED—PENALTY.

Section 1. Any person who shall use insulting and abusive language to and toward any teacher in or about any public school house, or who shall wilfully disturb any public school or district meeting, shall be deemed guilty of a misdemeanor, and, upon conviction, shall be fined in any sum not less than five dollars, and not exceeding one hundred dollars.

OFFENSES DEFINED—PENALTY—CONTINUED.

Sec. 2. Any person who shall wilfully break, cut, deface, despoil, injure, damage or destroy any school property, or who shall cut, mark, write or otherwise place or put on, or cause to be placed or put upon, any school property, any language or pictures or figures or signs of an obscene character, shall be deemed guilty of a misdemeanor, and, upon conviction thereof, shall pay a fine of not less than five dollars, nor more than one hundred dollars. The said fines shall be paid into the

*Note—The provision as to fees is repealed by Art. XIV of the Constitution and Laws of 1890-91, ch. 55.

treasury of the school district in which the offense was committed.

Chapter 3—Miscellaneous Provisions.

SCHOOL WEEK AND MONTH DEFINED.

Section 1. For the purposes of this act, a school week shall consist of five days; and a school month shall consist of all the days of a calendar month except Saturdays and Sundays, and legal holidays.

SCHOOL OFFICERS SHALL NOT SELL NOR ACT AS AGENT FOR
SCHOOL SUPPLIES—PENALTY.

Sec. 2. Neither the Territorial Superintendent, nor any person in his office, nor any County Superintendent, nor school district officer, nor any officer or teacher connected with any public school, shall act as agent or solicitor for the sale of any school books, maps, charts, school library books, school furniture, apparatus or stationery, or furnish any assistance to, or receive any reward therefor from, any author, publisher, bookseller, or dealer, doing the same. Every person violating this section shall forfeit not less than fifty nor more than two hundred dollars for each offense, and be liable to removal from office therefor.

TERRITORIAL TREASURER SHALL KEEP SCHOOL FUND.

Sec. 3. The Territorial Treasurer shall keep a separate fund, to be known as the "school fund," and all moneys appropriated for school purposes shall be kept in such fund.

SCHOOL DISTRICTS MAY ACQUIRE REALTY—CONDEMNATION.

Sec. 4. Every school district shall have the power to acquire, by purchase, donation or condemnation, any real estate situate within the district, as a site for any public school house or school grounds, and shall have power, when the interests of the district demand, as manifested by a majority of the electors of the district at any regular meeting, or at any special meeting called for the purpose, to condemn any public or private real estate, including highways, streets and alleyways, and to take therein the fee simple absolute, which power of condemnation shall be exercised in the manner prescribed by law for the condemnation of real estate by railroad corporations.

Chapter 4.

COUNTY TEACHERS' INSTITUTE.

Section 1. The County Superintendent of Public Schools shall hold annually, at some convenient place, a County Teachers' Institute for the instruction and advancement of teachers. Said Institute shall continue not less than four days nor more than five days. The County Superintendent shall preside at all meetings and determine the time and place for holding such Institute. It shall be the duty of all teachers actually engaged in teaching in such county to atend such Institute, unless they shall have a written excuse, signed by the County Superintendent. It shall be the duty of each district Board to pay all teachers who attend such Institute the same salary per day they would have paid had the same amount of time been spent in teaching. It shall be the duty of the County Board of Commissioners, in each county, to appropriate annually the sum of one hundred dollars for the payment of such instructors or lecturers as the County Superintendent may employ to assist him in holding the County Institute.

REPEALING SECTIONS 3909-3913, R. S. OF WYOMING.

Sec. 2. Sections thirty-nine hundred and nine, thirty-nine hundred and ten, thirty-nine hundred and eleven, thirty-nine hundred and twelve and thirty-nine hundred and thirteen of the Revised Statutes of Wyoming are hereby repealed.

ADOPTION AND USE OF TEXT BOOKS.

Sec. 3. At the expiration of the period of five years for which the books now in use are adopted, the County Superintendents and City Superintendents of Schools in the Territory shall meet at a call of the Territorial Superintendent of Public Instruction to adopt a series of text books, and the books thus adopted shall be the only legal text books to be used in the public schools of the Territory for the ensuing five years.

REPEAL OF INCONSISTENT ACTS.

Sec. 4. All acts and parts of acts inconsistent with the provisions of this act, be and the same are hereby repealed.

IN FORCE.

Sec. 5. This act shall take effect and be in force from and after its passage.

(Approved March 9, 1888.)

CHAPTER 17, (Laws 1888, p. 27.)

DISPOSAL OF REVISED STATUTES.

An Act regulating the sale of Revised Statutes.

Be it enacted by the Council and House of Representatives of the Territory of Wyoming:

(EXTRACT.)

TERRITORIAL LIBRARIAN SHALL CONTROL.

Section 1. The Revised Statutes of Wyoming, published in 1887, shall be distributed, sold and disposed of by the Terriaorial Librarian in the manner by this act, and not otherwise.

DISTRIBUTION.

Sec. 2. All Territorial, county and precinct officers and Clerks of school districts, and members of the Legislative Assembly, shall be supplied with copies of the Revised Statutes, free of cost, except as otherwise hereinafter provided.

*   *   *   *   *

REQUISITION FOR, COUNTY OFFICERS.

Sec. 4. The several County Clerks of the organized counties shall, from time to time, make a requisition upon the Territorial Librarian for as many copies of the Revised Statutes as may be actually required for the use of the officers in their respective counties.   *   *   *

DISTRIBUTION BY COUNTY CLERK.

Sec. 5. The County Clerk shall distribute one copy of the Revised Statutes to each county and precinct officer in his county who does not at the time possess a copy of the Revised Statutes; and the County Clerk shall take a receipt from every officer to whom he shall so deliver a copy of said Statutes.

*   *   *   *   *

(From the Revised Statutes—amended.)

PAYMENT OF TAXES—WHAT RECEIVABLE FOR TAXES.

Sec. 3815, (as amended and re-enacted by laws of 1890·

1891, ch. 16, page 118). "State warrants are receivable for the full amount of taxes payable into the State treasury. Money only is receivable at the county treasury of the proper county for poll tax, school tax, and the payment of bonded indebtedness or the interest thereon. All other county taxes may be paid in county warrants of the county for which taxes are paid. When a State or county warrant of any kind is received for the payment of taxes by the County Treasurer, he shall endorse upon it the name of the person from whom it was received, the amount for which it was received, and the date when received, and from that date the warrant shall be cancelled and shall not be re-issued. But when the county warrant amounts to more than is to be paid by the person presenting it for the payment of taxes, the Treasurer shall give him a certificate of the balance due after payment of taxes, which certificate shall entitle the holder thereof to another warrant on the same fund as the original warrant, on presentation of such certificate to the Board of County Commissioners."

(Approved December 24, 1890.)

MALFEASANCE OF PUBLIC OFFICER.

Sec. 966. Every Clerk, Sheriff, Collector, Treasurer, Assessor or other Territorial, county, district, township, city, town or school officer, or deputy of either, who shall be guilty of any palpable omission of duty, as such officer, or who shall wilfully or corruptly be guilty of oppression or partiality in the discharge of his official duties, or who shall demand or receive pay for services not authorized to be performed by him as such officer, or shall demand or receive pay for the performance of the duties, or supposed duties, of any public officer, unless duly authorized in writing to perform the duties of such officer in his place and stead, shall be guilty of malfeasance and shall, upon conviction thereof, be fined in a sum not exceeding two hundred dollars, and the court shall have power, upon the recommendation of the jury, to add to the judgment of the court, that any officer so convicted shall be removed from office. The court shall have power, whenever any Clerk of the District Court or Prosecuting Attorney shall be presented or indicted, to appoint for that occasion a Prosecuting Attorney or Clerk, as the case may require, who shall thereby be invested, in relation to such presentment or indictment, with all the powers of Clerk or Prosecuting Attorney. It shall be the duty of the court, when judgment shall extend to removal from office, to cause immediate notice of such removal to be given to the proper department, in order that the vacancy thus occasioned may be filled. (C. L. 1876, ch. 35, sec. 96.)

APPLICATION BY SURETY OF SCHOOL DISTRICT TREASURER.

Sec. 3046. A surety of the Treasurer of school funds in any school district, organized under the provisions of law, may at any time notify the Board of County Commissioners of the proper county, by giving at least five days' notice in writing, that he is unwilling to continue as surety for such treasurer, and will, at a time therein named, make application to the Board of County Commissioners to be released from further liability upon his bond; and he shall also give at least three days' notice in writing to such treasurer, of the time and place at which the application will be made. (S. L. 1885, ch. 60, sec. 698, R. S. O., sec. 5841.)

PROCEEDINGS BY COMMISSIONERS IN SUCH CASE.

Sec. 3047. The Board of County Commissioners, upon such notice being given, shall hear the application, and if in their opinion there is good reason therefor, shall require the Treasurer to give a new bond, conditioned according to law and to the satisfaction of the Board, within such time as they may direct, and if the Treasurer fail to execute such bond, the office shall be deemed vacant and shall be immediately filled as other vacancies therein; but such original sureties shall not be released or discharged until the filing of the new bond or the expiration of the time allowed therefor; and the cost of such application shall be paid by the person making the same. (S. L. 1886, ch. 60, sec. 699. R. S. O., sec. 5842.)

ENUMERATION OF LEGAL HOLIDAYS.

Sec. 1430. The first day of January, the twenty-second day of February, the thirtieth day of May, the fourth day of July, the day that may be appointed by the President of the United States as the annual Thanksgiving day, and the twenty-fifth day of December of each and every year are hereby declared legal holidays in and for the Territory of Wyoming (S. L. 1886, ch. 67, sec. 1.)

CHAPTER   43,   (Laws 1890-1891, p. 175).

CERTIFICATES UPON BONDS, ETC., RESPECTING DEBT LIMIT.

*   *   *   *   *

CERTIFICATE OF CLERK OF SCHOOL DISTRICT ON BONDS.

Sec. 2.   The Clerk of each school district of each county shall endorse a certificate upon every bond or evidence of debt issued pursuant to law, that the same is within the lawful debt limit of such school district, and is issued according to law. He shall sign such certificate in his official character.

*   *   *   *   *

(Approved January 9, 1891.)

CHAPTER 3.

BLIND, DEAF AND DUMB INSTITUTE.

CREATION OF INSTITUTE—LIMITATION.

Sec. 3725.   There shall be located and permanently maintained, at the City of Cheyenne, in the County of Laramie, an institute for the support and education of the blind, deaf and dumb; Provided, That no institute shall be opened until there are twelve pupils ready and that will enter said school, and when the number of pupils shall fall below the number of eight, then said institute shall close. (S. L. 1886, ch. 77, sec. 1.)

BOND OF TRUSTEES.

Sec. 3726, (amended—see note following this chapter). Said institute shall be under the supervision of a Board of Trustees, consisting of three persons, who shall be appointed by the Governor and confirmed by the Territorial Council; said Trustees shall hold office for two years, and until their successors are appointed and qualified, subject to removal for cause. When a vacancy occurs in said Board, by death, resignation or removal, and if the Council shall not be in session, the Governor shall have power to fill such vacancy by appointment. (S. L. 1886, ch. 77, sec. 2.)

ORGANIZATION OF BOARD.

Sec. 3727. Said Trustees shall meet at the City of Cheyenne, within one month from the date of their appointment, for the purpose of organization. They shall choose one of their number for President, and another for Secretary of said Board. In the absence of the President, a President pro tempore may be named to perform the duties of President. Two of said Trustees shall constitute a quorum for the transaction of business. (S. L. 1886, ch. 77, sec. 3.)

OATH OF TRUSTEES—DUTIES OF PRESIDENT AND SECRETARY.

Sec. 3728. Each member of said Board shall, before entering upon his duties, take and subscribe an oath to support the Constitution of the United States, the organic act of this Territory, and that he will faithfully discharge the duties required of him by the provisions of this chapter. The President shall preside at all meetings of the Board when present, and sign all certificates of indebtedness, bills and all papers approved or allowed by said Board. The Secretary shall keep a correct record of the proceedings of the Board, and have charge of, in trust for the institute, all papers, records and accounts of the same. (S. L. 1886, ch. 77, sec. 4.)

POWERS OF TRUSTEES.

Sec. 3729. Said Board shall have the general supervision of the institute, adopt rules for the government thereof, employ officers, teachers and servants, provide necessaries for the institute, and perform all other acts necessary to render it efficient and to carry out the purposes of its establishment. (S. L. 1886, ch. 77, sec. 5.)

EXPENSES TO BE CONFINED TO APPROPRIATION.

Sec. 3730. The Board shall not create any indebtedness against the institute exceeding the amount appropriated by the Legislature for the use thereof. (S. L. 1886, ch. 77, sec. 6.)

PAYMENT OF EXPENSES—COMPENSATION OF TRUSTEES.

Sec. 3731. All indebtedness incurred by said Board in carrying out the provisions of this chapter, together with the compensation of five dollars per day for the time actually employed in such services, and also the necessary traveling expenses of each, shall be paid out of the Territorial treasury upon a certificate of the President of the Board, stating the items of such indebtedness, expenses and compensation, and that the same is just and necessary, according to he provisions of this chapter, and upon the presentation of said certificate to the Auditor of the Territory, he shall issue his warrant or warrants to the party or parties to whom such money is due and payable, and the Territorial Treasurer shall pay such warrants out of any moneys appropriated for that purpose. But the Auditor shall not issue any warrant without an itemized account, properly sworn to, accompanying the certificate of the President of the Board. Said accounts may be sworn to before the President of said Board, who is hereby authorized and empowered to administer oaths for that purpose. (S. L. 1886, ch. 77, sec, 7.)

INMATES NOT RESIDENTS OF TERRITORY.

Sec. 3732. Persons not residents of this Territory, of suitable age and capacity, shall be entitled to an education in said institute on paying to the Territorial Treasurer the sum of three hundred dollars per annum, in advance. (S. L. 1886, ch. 77, sec. 8.)

WHO ADMITTED TO INSTITUTE.

Sec. 3733. Every blind, deaf or dumb person, who is a resident of this Territory, of suitable age and capacity, shall be entitled to receive an education in said institute at the expense of the Territory. (S. L. 1886, ch. 77, sec. 9.)

ASSESSOR TO REPORT NAMES OF AFFLICTED.

Sec. 3734. The County Assessor of each county shall annually report to the County Clerk the names, ages, postoffice address and names of parents or guardians, of every blind, deaf or dumb person between the ages of seven and twenty-

4

one years, residing in his county, including all such persons as may be too deaf to acquire an education in the common schools. The County Clerk shall, on or before the first day of August in each year, send a list containing the names, ages and residences of all such persons to the principal of the institute. S. L. 1886, ch. 77, sec. 10.)

PUPILS TO BE PROPERLY CLOTHED—PAYMENT OF EXPENSE

Sec. 3735. When the pupils of said institute are not otherwise supplied with clothing, they shall be furnished by the principal, who shall make out an account of the cost thereof in each case against the parent or guardian, and against the pupil if he or she have no parent or guardian, which account shall be certified to be correct by the principal, and when so certified such an account shall be presumed to be correct in all courts. The principal shall thereupon remit such accounts by mail to the Treasurer of the county from which the pupil so supplied shall have come to said institute. Such Treasurer shall proceed at once to collect the same by suit in the name of his county, if necessary, and pay the same into the Terri torial treasury; the principal shall at the same time remit a duplicate of such account to the Auditor of the Territory, who shall credit the same to the account of the institute, and charge it to the proper county; Provided, If it shall appear by the affidavit of three disinterested citizens of the county, not akin to the pupil, that the said pupil or his or her parents would be unreasonably oppressed by such suit, then such Treasurer shall not commence the said suit, but shall credit the same to the Territory on his books, and report the amount of such account to the Board of Commissioners of his county, and the said Board shall, out of the general fund of said county, cause the same to be paid into the Territorial treasury. (S. L. 1886, ch. 77, sec. 11.)

OFFICERS AND THEIR DUTIES.

Sec. 3736. The officers of the institute shall be a principal and a matron. The principal shall be a resident officer of the same. He shall annually certify to the Board of Trustees a written report, stating in full the true condition of the educational, the domestic and the industrial departments of the institute, his action and proceedings therein. He shall keep and have charge of the necessary records, register and accounts of said departments; have supervision of its teachers, pupils and servants, and perform such other duties as the Board may require. He shall quarterly certify to the Board a full and written report of all his expenditures. He shall secure and employ all assistants needed therein, with the consent and approval of the Board. He shall have special charge of the male pupils out of school hours, and shall furnish them with employment about the premises, or in some trade to which they are adapted. The products and proceeds arising from the labor and employment of all the pupils shall inure to the use and benefit of the institute. (S. L. 1886, ch. 77, sec. 12.)

DUTIES OF MATRON.

Sec. 3737. The matron of the institute shall also be a resident officer of the same. She shall have control of the internal management of the house, and of the female pupils out of school hours; she shall instruct them in and about the house, and the domestic departments, or in some trade to which they are adapted. under the direction of the principal. (S. L. 1886, ch. 77, sec. 13.)

PRESIDENT TO MAKE ANNUAL REPORT TO GOVERNOR.

Sec. 3738. The President of the Board of Trustees shall, on or before the first day of December in each year, make out to the Governor of the Territory a full and complete report, as follows, to-wit:

First—A statement of the financial condition of the institute from the date of the last report, giving in detail the amount of moneys received from all sources, and the amount expended;

Second—The value of real estate at date of last report, and cost of improvements made, if any, since last report;

Third—The number of pupils in attendance, also the number that have entered and the number of those who may have left it since last report;

Fourth—The number of deaths, if any, that have occurred in the institute since last report;

Fifth—The improvement, health and discipline of the pupils;

Sixth—The number of officers, teachers and servants employed, with the salary of each;

Seventh—All other needful information touching every point that may be deemed of interest to be communicated. (S. L. 1886, ch. 77, sec. 14.)

PROVISION FOR TEMPORARY CARE OF BLIND, DEAF AND DUMB.

Note—Under chap. 15, laws 1890-91, approved December 24. 1890. temporary provision is made, until the opening of the State Blind, Deaf and Dumb Institute for the care of the blind, deaf and dumb, and an appropriation of seven hundred and fifty dollars is made for this purpose.   ....

INSTITUTE TRANSFERRED TO CONTROL OF STATE BOARD OF CHARITIES AND REFORM.

Under the provision of sec. 2, chap. 37, laws of 1890-1891, approved January 8th, 1891, general supervision and control of the Deaf, Dumb and Blind Institute at Cheyenne, Wyo., is transferred to the State Board of Charities and Reform, comprising the State Treasurer, State Auditor, and State Superintendent of Public Instruction, by whom deaf, dumb and blind persons within the State are now being educated in institutions of other States until such time as the number of persons requiring such tuition shall be sufficient to enable the State institution to be opened and put in operation as provided by the law creating it.

CHAPTER 35.

AOPTION OF REVISED STATUTES, AND SESSION LAWS OF 1888 AND 1890.

*   *   *   *   *

REVISED STATUTES AND LAWS OF 1888 AND 1890, ARE LAWS OF STATE IF NOT IN CONFLICT WITH CONSTITUTION EXCEPT AS REPEALED OR AMENDED.

Section 1.   That all of the Revised Statutes, and Session Laws of the years eighteen hundred and eighty-eight and eighteen hundred and ninety of the Territory (now State) of Wyoming, in so far as they do not conflict with, and are not repugnant to, the provisions of the Constitution of the State of Wyoming, be and the same are hereby declared to be in full force and effect, and they are hereby made the laws of the State of Wyoming, except in so far as they may have been or may be repealed, or amended and re-enacted, by the Legislature of Wyoming.

CONFLICTING ACTS REPEALED.

Sec. 2.   All acts and parts of acts in conflict with this act are hereby repealed

Sec. 3.   This act shall take effect and be in force from and after its passage.

Approved January 8, 1891.

UNIVERSITY OF WYOMING.

Note--The laws relating to the issue and payment of the University building bonds are herein omitted.

An Act of Incorporation.

An Act to amend so much of chapter one, title forty-two, of the Revised Statutes of Wyoming, as relates to the establishment, government and maintenance of the University of Wyoming:

Be it enacted by the Legislature of the State of Wyoming:

That so much of chapter one of title forty-two of the Revised Statutes of Wyoming as relates to the establishment, government and maintenance of the University of Wyoming is hereby amended so as to read as follows:

Section 1. There is established in this State, at the City of Laramie, an institution of learning under the name and style of the "University of Wyoming."

Sec. 2. The objects of such University shall be to provide an efficient means of imparting to young men and young women, without regard to color, on equal terms, a liberal education, together with a thorough knowledge of the various branches connected with the scientific, industrial and professional pursuits. To this end it shall embrace colleges or departments of letters, of science and of the arts, together with such professional or other departments as in the course of time may be connected therewith. The department of letters shall embrace a liberal course of instruction in language, literature and philosophy, together with such courses or parts of courses in the college or department of science as are deemed necessary.

The college or department of science shall embrace courses of instruction in the mathematical, physical and natural sciences, together with such courses in language, literature and philosophy as shall constitute a liberal education. The college or department of arts shall embrace courses of instruction in the practical and fine arts; especially in the application of science to the arts of mining and metallurgy, mechanics, engineering, architecture, agriculture and commerce, together with instruction in military tactics and in such branches in the department of letters as are necessary to a proper fitness of students for their chosen pursuits, and as soon as the income of the University shall allow, in such order as the wants of the public shall seem to require, the said courses in the sciences and their practical applications shall be expanded into full and distinct schools and departments.

Sec. 3. The government of the University shall rest in a board of nine Trustees to be appointed by the Governor, three, and only three, of whom shall at all times be residents of the County of Albany; together with the President of the University and the State Superintendent of Public Instruction, as members, ex-officio, as such having the right to speak but not to vote.

The term of office of the Trustees appointed shall be six years, except as provided in the next succeeding section.

Sec. 4. It shall be the duty of the Governor, during the present session of the Legislature, to nominate, and by and with the advice and consent of the Senate to appoint, nine residents of the State as members of the said Board of Trustees; three of whom shall serve for two years, three of whom shall serve for four years, and three of whom shall serve for six years; and thereafter during the session of each succeeding Legislature the Governor shall nominate, and by and with the advice and consent of the Senate, appoint successors to those of said Trustees whose term of office shall have expired, or will expire before the next session of the Legislature. Any vacancy in the Board of Trustees caused by death, resignation or removal from the State, or otherwise, shall be filled by appointment to be made by the Governor, which appointment shall continue until the next session of the Legislature, and no longer, "but no member of the Faculty, while holding that position, shall be appointed a Trustee."

Sec. 5. The Board of Trustees and their successors in office shall constitute a body corporate by the name of "The Trustees of the University of Wyoming." They shall possess all the powers necessary or convenient to accomplish the objects and perform the duties prescribed by law, and shall have the custody of the books, records, buildings and all other property of the University. The Board shall have power to elect a President, Secretary and Treasurer, who shall perform such duties as are prescribed in the by-laws of the Board. The Treasurer shall execute such bond, with approved sureties, in double the sum likely to come into his hands, for the faithful discharge of his duties, as the Board shall require. The term of office of said officers, their duties severally, and the times of holding meetings, shall be fixed in the by-laws of the Board. A majority of the Board shall constitute a quorum for the transaction of business, but a less number may adjourn from time to time, and all routine business may be entrusted to an executive committee of three members, subject to such conditions as the by-laws of the Board shall prescribe. The actual and necessary traveling expenses of non-resident members in attending the annual meeting of the Board may be audited by the Auditing Committee thereof and paid by warrants on the Treasurer out of the general fund of the University.

Sec. 6. The Board of Trustees shall prescribe rules for the government of the University in all its branches, elect the requisite officers, professors, instructors and employes, any of whom may be removed for cause, as well as fix the salary and term of office of each, prescribe the studies to be pursued and the text books to be used, and determine the qualifications of applicants for admission to the various courses of study; but no instruction, either sectarian in religion or partisan in politics, shall ever be allowed in any department of the University, and no sectarian or partisan test shall ever be exercised or allowed in the appointment of Trustees, or in the election or removal of professors, teachers or other officers of the University, or in the admission of students thereto, or for any purpose whatever. The Board of Trustees shall have the power to confer such degrees and grant such diplomas as are usual in universities, or as they shall deem appropriate; through by-laws, to confer upon the Faculty the power to suspend or expel students for causes therein prescribed; to possess and use for the benefit of the institution all property of the University; to hold, manage, lease, or dispose of, according to law, any real or personal estate, as shall be conducive to the welfare of the institution; to expend the income placed under their control, from whatever source derived; and, finally, to exercise any and all other functions properly belonging to such a Board and necessary to the prosperity of the University in all of its departments.

Sec. 7. At the close of each fiscal year the Trustees, through their President, shall make a report in detail to the Governor, exhibiting the progress, condition and wants of the University, and of each school or department thereof, the course of study in each, the number of professors and students, the amount of receipts and disbursements, together with the nature, costs and results of all important investigations, and such other information as they may deem important or as may be required by any law of this State or of the United States.

Sec. 8. The President and professors of the University shall be styled "The Faculty," and shall have power, as such body, to enforce the rules and regulations adopted by the

Trustees for the government of students, to reward and censure students as they may deserve, and generally to exercise such discipline, in harmony with the said regulations, as shall be necessary to the good order of the institution; to present to the Trustees for degrees and honors such students as are entitled thereto, and in testimony thereof when ordered by the Board, suitable diplomas, certificates, or other testimonials, under seal of the University and the signatures of the Faculty. When, in course of time, distinct colleges or departments of the University are duly organized and in active operation, the immediate government of such departments shall, in like manner, be entrusted to their respective faculties.

Sec. 9. The President of the University shall be President of the several faculties and the executive head of all the departments. As such, subject to the Board of Trustees, he shall have authority to give general direction to the instruction and investigations of the several schools and departments, and so long as the interests of the institution require it, he may be charged with the duties of one of the professorships.

Sec. 10. To the end that none of the youth of the State who crave the benefits of higher education may be denied them, and that all may be encouraged to avail themselves of the advantages offered by the University, tuition shall be as nearly free as possible, and it shall be wholly free to such students from each county as are selected and appointed by the Board of County Commissioners therein.

Sec. 11. After any student has graduated from either of the chief departments of the University, and received the degree of Bachelor of Arts, of Letters, of Philosophy or of Science, and has had a subsequent expeerience as a successful teacher of a public school in Wyoming for a period of one school year, the State Superintendent of Public Instruction shall have authority to countersign the diploma of such teacher after such examination as to moral character, learning and ability to teach, as to the said Superintendent may seem proper; and such graduate so tested shall, after his diploma has been countersigned by the State Superintendent as aforesaid, be qualified to teach in any of the public schools of this State; and the diploma so countersigned shall be his certificate for such qualification until annulled by the State Superintendent of Public Instruction.

Sec. 12. In order that the University may be kept "in a condition of full efficiency," as required by the terms of section sixteen of article seven of the Constitution of the State of Wyoming, there shall be assessed upon all taxable property of the State in each year, as heretofore, a tax of one-eighth of a mill on each and every dollar of the assessed valuation of such property, which tax shall be levied, collected and paid to the State Treasurer in the manner provided by law for the levy, collection and payment of other State taxes. Said tax, when so paid to the State Treasurer, shall be paid to the Treasurer of the said Board of Trustees upon the warrant of the State Auditor, to be issued upon request of said Board of Trustees.

Sec. 13. "The University of Wyoming" having been designated by the Secretary of the Interior as the proper institution to receive and expend the moneys appropriated by an act of Congress, approved August thirtieth, eighteen hundred and ninety, entitled, "An act to apply a portion of the proceeds of the public lands to the more complete endowment and support of colleges for the benefit of agriculture and the mechanic arts, established under the provisions of an act of Congress, approved July second, eighteen hundred and sixty-two," until such time as there may be an agricultural college established in this State, separate and apart from the said University of Wyoming, assent is hereby given to all the terms and conditions of said act of Congress, and grants of money, authorized and made by said act, by the act of March second, eighteen hundred and eighty-seven, relative to the establishment of agricultural experiment stations, or any other act for like purposes, are hereby assented to and accepted by the State of Wyoming. Except where other designation is made by Congress, all moneys granted or donated by Congress in aid of scientific instruction or experimentation, and set apart by the Legislature for such use by the University of Wyoming, shall be accepted and received by the State Treasurer, and by him placed at the disposal of the Board of Trustees of the said University by transfer to the Treasurer of said Board, for disbursement in accordance with the provisions of the act or acts of Congress aforesaid.

Sec. 14. All acts and parts of acts inconsistent with the provisions of this act are hereby repealed.

Sec. 15. This act shall take effect and be in force from and after its passage.

Approved January 10th, 1891.

CHAPTER 32.

An Act prescribing the age at which deaf and dumb children
may be admitted as pupils in the Blind, Deaf and Dumb
Asylum, as State charges.

Be it enacted by the Legislature of the State of Wyoming:

Section 1. That deaf and dumb children of the age of
nine years and over shall be admitted as inmates to the Blind
and Deaf and Dumb Asylum of this State, when the same shall
be opened for the education and support of the blind, deaf and
dumb, and until such time it shall be the duty of the Board of
Trustees of said institution or the State Board of Charities to
provide for the support, maintenance and education of deaf and
dumb children of the age of nine years and over, in such asylum
as has been selected for the support, maintenance and education
of other blind, deaf and dumb of this State, as provided in
chapter 15 of the Laws of Wyoming, 1890-91, entitled, "Blind,
Deaf and Dumb."

Sec. 2. This act shall take effect and be in force from and
after its passage.

Approved February 18, 1893.

CHAPTER 10.

REFUNDING BONDS IN SCHOOL DISTRICTS.

An Act providing for the issuing of refunding bonds in school
districts.

Be it enacted by the Legislature of the State of Wyoming:

Section 1. The Board of Directors of each and every
school district in the State of Wyoming, are hereby authorized
to issue refunding bonds of such school district, for the purpose
of taking up outstanding bonds of such school district, for any
sum not exceeding the amount of outstanding bonds; Provided,
That the qualified electors of any such school district shall so
elect and determine at any regular meeting or at any special
meeting, held for that purpose.

Sec. 2. Said bonds shall be issued in sums of not less than one hundred dollars, and shall be redeemed by the schol district issuing the same within a period not exceeding thirty years, and not less than five years from the date of issue, and shall bear interest at a rate not exceeding six per centum per annum on each dollar of their face, which interest shall be payable annually or semi-annually, the rate of interest to be determined by the Board of Schol Directors. Such bonds shall be numbered from one upwards, and be headed, "Refunding bonds of school district number ———— in the county of ————————, State of Wyoming;" and before being issued shall be registered by the Treasurer of the county within which such school district is situated.

Sec. 3. The County Treasurer of each county shall keep a book in which shall be registered all such bonds, showing the number of the bond, the date of issue, amount, number of coupons, date of redemption, date of registry and payment of interest on such bonds, which book shall, during business hours, be open for inspection.

Sec. 4. All bonds issued by virtue of this act shall be signed by the presiding officer of the Board of Directors of such school district, countersigned by the County Treasurer of the county in which such school district is situated, and attested by the Clerk of such school district, with the seal of such school district attached; and none of such bonds shall be sold for less than their face value, and shall not be sold until thirty days' notice shall have been given in some newspaper of general circulation in the State of Wyoming.

Sec. 5. Said bonds shall have coupons attached, representing the interest to be paid each year, and the coupons representing said interest shall be detached from the bonds before presentation for payment of the interest for the year corresponding, and upon payment shall be forthwith cancelled by the County Treasurer, by writing the word "cancelled" across the face thereof. The interest on all such bonds shall be payable at the office of the County Treasurer of the county in which such school district issuing such bonds is situated, or in any place designated by the Board of School Directors of such school district.

Sec. 6. There shall be annually levied by the Board of County Commissioners of the county within which is situate any school district issuing any such bonds, as are in this act provided for, on all taxable property within the limits of said school district, a tax not to exceed seven mills on the dollar of valuation, which shall be known as the Refunding Bond Fund of school district No. ————. Said tax shall be payable only in the lawful money of the United States, and shall be used to pay the interest and principal of said bonds, and for no other purpose; and said tax shall be collected in the same manner and at the same time as the county taxes, and paid into the county treasury by the collector of taxes.

Sec. 7. The Board of School Directors of any school district, which may issue bonds as provided in this act, shall, each year after the tenth year, retire as many of such bonds as can be redeemed with the amount of said bond fund at the time in the hands of the County Treasurer, and in all such cases such bonds shall be redeemed by the payment of number one first, and proceeding continuously upwards with those outstanding. All cancelled bonds shall be turned over to the Board of Directors at such times as they may direct.

Sec. 8. That all taxable property of any school district, issuing bonds as herein provided for at the time of issuing such bonds, shall be a pledge to the payment of the principal and interest of such bonds in the manner herein provided, and it shall not be lawful to use or divert any portion of such bond fund for any purpose whatever, except for the payment of said principal and interest, and as provided in section six of this act.

Sec 9. The County Treasurer of each county in which any school district, issuing bonds as herein provided for, is situated, shall have custody of all funds realized from the sale of such bonds and shall pay the same out only upon the return of such bonds for the redemption of which the refunding bonds, for the issue of which this act provides, may have been issued. Such bonds so redeemed shall be cancelled by the County Treasurer and turned over to the Board of School Directors of the school district which issued said redeemed bonds, at such time as they may direct. It shall be the duty of the County Treasurer to give a separate bond to be made to such school district, in such sum and with such sureties as the Board of County Commissioners of the county may deem proper and sufficient, conditioned for the faithful accounting of the moneys deposited with him and realized from the sale of such bonds as are herein provided for, and such Treasurer's separate bond shall be and remain in the custody of the County Clerk of the county in which such school district is situated.

, Sec. 10. This act shall take effect and be in force from and after its passage.

Approved February 10, 1893.

CHAPTER 10.

REFUNDING BONDS IN SCHOOL DISTRICTS.

An Act supplemental to an act entitled, "An act providing for the issuing of refunding bonds in school districts," passed by the Second State Legislature, being Chapter 10, Session Laws of 1893, and to provide for any surplus funds realized by the sale of bonds authorized by said act, or remaining in the funds provided by law for the payment of the principal and interest of the bonds refunded by the authority of said act.

Be it enacted by the Legislature of the State of Wyoming:

FUNDS REALIZED FROM SALE OF BONDS—HOW USED.

Section 1. That whenever any school district shall have issued its refunding bonds in accordance with Chapter 10 of the Session Laws of the Second State Legislature, and the funds realized from the sale of such refunding bonds by reason of such bonds selling for more than their par value, are more than sufficient to redeem all the bonds, to redeem which said refunding bonds were issued, such surplus may be used, First: To pay all the expenses of issuing and disposing of said refunding bonds. Second: Any surplus still remaining shall be turned by the county treasurer into the "Refunding Bond Fund" of such school district and used for the purposes for which such fund is used as provided in Sec. six (6), of Chapter ten (10), of the Session Laws of the Second State Legislature.

BALANCE IN THE HANDS OF COUNTY TREASURER—HOW USED.

Sec. 2. Whenever any school district shall have issued its refunding bonds in accordance with the provisions of Chapter 10 of the Session Laws of the Second State Legislature and there remains in the hands of the county treasurer of the county in which said school district is situated any moneys belonging to the funds provided by law for the payment of the principal or interest or both of the bonds to redeem which said refunding bonds were issued, said money may be used, First: To pay any deficiency in the expenses of issuing

and disposing of said refunding bonds that cannot be paid by
the surplus realized from the sale of said refunding bonds as
provided for in Section 1 of this Act; Second: Any moneys
still remaining in said fund shall be turned by said county
treasurer into the "Refunding Bond Fund" of such school
district and used for the purposes for which such fund is used,
as provided in Sec. six (6) of Chapter (10) of the Session
Laws of the Second State Legislature.

SURPLUS—HOW USED.

Sec. 3. The county treasurer of any county in which is
situated a school district that may issue its refunding bonds
as provided in said Chapter ten (10) of the Session Laws of the
Second State Legislature, is hereby authorized and required
to pay out the surplus moneys derived from the sale of any
such refunding bonds referred to in Section 1 of this Act, or
te surplus moneys remaining in the old fund referred to in
Sec. 2 of this Act for the expenses incurred by such school
district in issuing and disposing of such refunding bonds on
orders of the school board of such school district, which
orders shall state on their face that the money to be so paid
was a legitimate expense incurred in the issue and sale of such
refunding bonds. When all of such expense has been paid
by the issue of such orders or otherwise the board of directors
shall over the seal of said district notify said county treasurer
of the fact that all the expense incurred in the issue and sale
of such refundin bonds has been paid whereupon said
treasurer shall immediately transfer all moneys remaining
in his hands applicable to the payment of interest or principal
of the old bonds to the "Refunding Bond Fund" of such school
district, as provided in Sections 1 and 2 of this Act: Provided,
however, That all the bonds to redeem which said refunding
bonds were issued have already been paid.

Sec. 4. All Acts and parts of Acts in conflict with or
inconsistent with the provisions of this Act in so far as they
so conflict are hereby repealed.

Sec. 5. This Act shall take effect and be in force from
and after its passage.

Approved January 31, A. D. 1895.

CHAPTER 25.

DEAF AND DUMB CHILDREN.

An Act prescribing the age at which deaf and dumb children may be admitted as pupils in the Blind, Deaf and Dumb Asylum as State charges.

Be it enacted by the Legislature of the State of Wyoming:

WHAT CHILDREN ADMITTED TO THE STATE INSTITUTIONS.

Section 1. That deaf and dumb children of the age of six years and over shall be admitted an inmates to the Blind, Deaf and Dumb Asylum of this State, when the same shall be opened for the education and support of the blind, deaf and dumb, and until such time it shall be the duty of the Board of Trustees of said institution, or the State Board of Charities, to provided for the support, maintenance and education of deaf and dumb children of the age of six years and over, in such asylum as has been selected for the support, maintenance and education of other blind, deaf and dumb of this State as provided in Chapter 15 of the Laws of Wyoming, 1890-91, entitled, "Blind, Deaf and Dumb."

Sec. 2. This Act shall take effect and be in force from and after its passage.

Approved February 8, A. D. 1895.

CHAPTER 34.

STATE BOARD OF CHARITIES AND REFORM.

An Act to amend and re-enact Section 1 and Section 8 of an act entitled, "An act creating and establishing a State Board of Charities and Reform, and prescribing in part their duties, and to repeal all acts and parts of acts inconsistent herewith," approved January 8, 1891.

Be it enacted by the Legislature of the State of Wyoming:

AMENDMENT.

Section 1. That Section 1 of an act entitled, "An act

creating and establishing a State Board of Charities and Reform, and prescribing in part their duties, and to repeal all acts and parts of acts inconsistent herewith," approved January 8, 1891, be, and the same is hereby amended and re enacted so as to read as follows: "Section 1. That the Governor, the Secretary of State, the State Treasurer, the State Auditor and the State Superintendent of Public Instruction shall constitute and shall hereafter be known as the State Board of Charities and Reform."

GOVERNOR TO BE PRESIDENT OF THE BOARD.

Sec. 2. That Sec. 8 of said act be and the same is hereby amended and re-enacted so as to read as follows: "Sec. 8. The Board shall meet at least once in each month, on the first Monday thereof, for the transaction of business. The Governor shall be President of the Board, and it shall be his duty to sign all papers or documents that shall be approved, made or directed by the Board. Any three of the Board shall constitute a quorum for the transaction of any or all business at any regular or special meeting. and the Board may provide for a President pro tem, whose powers shall be defined by the Board.

REPEAL.

Sec. 3. All acts and parts of acts inconsistent with this act are hereby repealed.

WHEN IN FORCE.

Sec. 4. This act shall take effect and be in force from and after its passage.

Approved February 13th, A. D. 1895.

CHAPTER 44.

DISTRIBUTION OF SCHOOL MONEY—DUTIES OF COUNTY
SUPERINTENDENT.

An Act relating to the duties of County Superintendent of
Schools, for the distribution of poll tax and for other purposes, and to amend and re-enact Chapter sixty-seven of
the Session Laws of Wyoming for the year one thousand
eight hundred and eighty-eight, entitled, "An act to
amend Section thirty-nine hundred and fourteen of the
Revised Statutes of Wyoming," approved March ninth,
1888.

Be it enacted by the Legislature of the State of Wyoming:

Section 1. That Section one of Chapter sixty-seven of the
session laws of Wyoming for the year one thousand eight hundred and eighty-eight, entitled, "An Act to amend Section
three thousand nine hundred and fourteen of the Revised Statutes of Wyoming," approved March ninth, 1888, be .and the
same is hereby amended and re-enacted so as to read as follows:

Section 1. Section three thousand nine hundred and fourteen of the Revised Statutes of Wyoming is hereby amended
and re-enacted to read as follows:

Sec. 3914. The duties of the county superintendent of
schools shall be as follows: He shall on the first Monday of
October in each year, transmit to the superintendent of public
instruction a report, containing an abstract of the several
particulars set forth in the reports of the district clerks,
together with a statement of the financial affairs of his office,
and such suggestions as he shall think proper, relative to the
schools of his county; he shall distribute to the districts
within his county such blank forms, circulars and other communications as may be transmitted to him for that purpose,
by the superintendent of public instruction; on the first
Monday of December, annually, he shall apportion the county
school tax and all money in the county treasury, belonging to
the county school fund in the following manner: Each school
district in his county shall be apportioned the sum of one
hundred and fifty dollars for the payment of teachers in such
district, and all moneys remaining after such apportionment
shall be apportioned to each district pro rata, according to

5

the number of pupils in attendance at the schools of said district, reported to him by the several district clerks: Provided, always, That each, every and all poll taxes, levied and collected for school purposes, in each school district in this state, shall when collected by the county treasurer, be paid over to the treasurer of the school district in which the persons respectively reside, who paid such poll tax, and the said poll taxes shall not be divided among the school districts of the county pro rata to the number of scholars in such school district, but the poll taxes so collected from the inhabitants of each school district shall be paid to the treasurer of the district in which they severally reside, for the support of the schools of such district; no district shall be entitled to the amount of one hundred and fifty dollars, for the payment of teachers, besides the pro rata apportionment as provided in this section, when there are less than eight scholars, of school age, in said district; he shall record a statement of such apportionment in his office, and he shall also notify the county treasurer of the same; he shall immediately draw an order on the county treasurer, in favor of the treasurer of each district for the amount of its proportion, and transmit the same to the treasurer of the district: Provided, Such district treasurer shall have given his official bond, which draft the county treasurer shall pay to the district treasurer on presentation of the draft properly endorsed. Should no apportionment of the school funds of the county be made on the first Monday in December, as required in this section he may make an apportionment as soon thereafter as practicable, in the same manner as hereinbefore provided. He may also make a supplementary apportionment of the money in the county school fund at any time after the first Monday in December, prior to the first of the following June, and such supplementary apportionment shall be pro rata, according to the number of pupils in attendance in any and all schools in each district, as reported to him by the several district clerks in their last annual reports. He shall divide the county into school districts, and may alter and change the boundaries of districts thus formed, from time to time as the convenience of the inhabitants of the aforesaid district may require, and shall proceed to make such change at any time, when petitioned by two-thirds of the legal voters of any district: Provided that the number of districts in any county whose population is less than ten thousand, shall not exceed twenty-five; and in case the number of districts in any county at the passage of this Act exceeds the proportion above stated, it shall be the duty of the superintendent of such county, immediately after the passage of this Act to re-district such county in accordance herewith. And the county superintendent of schools shall abolish or join in a contiguous district, any school district in which no school has been maintained for twelve consecutive months, and all funds to the credit of such district so abolished or joined to another district, shall be returned to, and become a part of the general school fund of the county: Provided, that nothing in this Act shall be so construed as to prevent the county superintendent of schools from joining any school district (having less than eight pupils, to any other school district lying contiguous thereto, if, in the judgment of said superintendent, it will be to the benefit of the public schools, to so join such districts. He shall examine every person offering himself or herself as a teacher of public schools, and if in his opinion such person is qualified to teach a public school, shall give him or her a certificate authorizing him or her to teach a public school in his county for one year. Whenever practicable, the examinations of teachers shall be competitive and the certificate shall be granted according to the qualifications of the applicant. He shall have the general superintendence of the schools of his county, and shall visit each school at least once each term, and shall have power to dismiss all teachers he may find to be incompetent.

Sec. 2. This Act shall take effect and be in force from and after its passage.

Approved February 15, A. D. 1895.

CHAPTER 50.

PUBLIC KINDERGARTEN.

An Act entitled, An act giving power to the Board of Trustees of any school district to establish and maintain the kindergarten system of instruction in the public schools, at which children between the ages of four and six years may receive such instruction.

Be it enacted by the Legislature of the State of Wyoming:

POWER OF TRUSTEES.

Section 1. The board of trustees of any school district in this state shall have power to establish and maintain free

kindergarten schools in connection with the public
schools of their district, for the instruction of children
residing in such district and be tween the ages of four
and six years, and shall establish such courses of training,
study and discipline and such rules and regulations for the
government of such kindergarten schools as said board may
deem advisable; Provided, That the cost of establishing and
maintaining such kindergarten schools shall be paid from the
special school fund of said school district, and the gross sum to
be so expended by the said board for such kindergarten schools
shall be annually fixed and determined by the qualified electors
of such district at the annual meeting of such electors.

SHALL BE PART OF SCHOOL SYSTEM—TEACHERS.

The said kindergarten schools shall be a part of the public
school system and governed as far as practicable in the same
manner and by the same officers as is now or hereafter may
be provided by law for the government of the other public
schools of the state; Provided, however, That teachers of the
kindergarten schools shall be the holders of certificates or
diplomas from some reputable institution for the training of
kindergarten teachers, and shall pass such other examination
and possess such other qualifications as may be required by
the board of trustees of the district employing them.

PRESENT LAW NOT CHANGED IN REFERENCE TO APPORTION-
    MENT.   ....

And Provided, further, That nothing in this Act shall
be so construed as to in any manner change the law, as it
now exists, with reference to the taking of the census of the
school population or the apportionment of the state and county
school funds among the several counties and districts in this
state.

HOW CARRIED INTO EFFECT.

Sec. 2. That for the purpose of carrying into effect the
provisions of the foregoing section, it shall be lawful for the
qualified electors of any school district in the state at the
annual meeting held under the provisions of existing law to
vote such sum of money as may be necessary to establish and
maintain such kindergarten schools, during the school year
next following such meeting such sum in the aggregate, not
to exceed one mill upon the dollar of the valuation of the
property in the district as determined by the next preceding

annual assessment thereof for the purpose of taxation, the same to be certified, levied, collected and disbursed in the same manner as is now provided by law with respect to the special school funds of the several school districts in this state.

WHEN ACT TAKES EFFECT.

Sec. 3. This Act shall be in force and effect from and after its passage.

Approved February 15, A. D. 1895.

CHAPTER 53.

DISTRIBUTION OF SCHOOL FUNDS.

An Act to provide for the distribution of the income derived from the investment of the permanent school funds and from the leasing of State school lands. z

Be it enacted by the Legislature of the State of Wyoming:

REFERENCE TO LAST PRECEDING REPORTS OF COUNTY SUPERINTENDENTS.

Section 1. On or before the thirty-first day of March in each year, if there shall be any money to the credit of the income fund, for the use of public schools in the state treasury, including the rents of the unsold school lands, the state superintendent of public instruction shall distribute such income among the several counties of the state accordng to the number of children of school age in each, the same to be determined by reference to the last preceding annual reports furnished to the state superintendent of public instruction by the several county superintendents of schools. Such moneys so distributed shall be paid to the county treasurer of each county by the state treasurer, upon the requisition to that effect by the state superintendent of public instruction, which said requisition shall state the county entitled thereto, together with the amount, and the fund out of which it is to be paid; and the superintendent of public instruppction shall at the same time notify each superintendent of schools that such distribution has been made; such requisition shall be accompanied by a warrant of the auditor upon the treasurer covering the

amount of the requisition in each case, and the superintendent
of public instruction shall file such requisition with the auditor
and a copy of the same with the treasurer. Upon such distribution being made and said money being paid to the respective
county treasurers, the county superintendent of schools in
each county shall cause such money to be distributed among
the several school districts in the county pro rata in the same
manner and in the same proportion as the regular county school
tax is required by law to be distributed. Provided, however that
any law with reference to the distribution of the county school
tax which provides for a certain amount to be paid to each
school district before the pro rata distribution of the balance
is made shall not apply in the case of the distribution of the
said moneys under this Act. Provided, further, that no
apportionment from said state fund shall be made to any
school district for a year in which a school has not been maintained therein for at least three months.

Sec. 2. This Act shall take effect and be in force from
and after January 1, 1896.

Approved February 16, A. D. 1895.

CHAPTER 67.

INVESTMENT OF LAND FUNDS.

An Act to provide for the investment of the permanent funds
arising from the sale of State lands.

Be it enacted by the Legislature of the State of Wyoming:

APPROVAL OF GOVERNOR AND ATTORNEY GENERAL.

Section 1. All permanent funds arising from the sale of
State lands and any permanent addition thereto may, and
whenever practicable, shall be invested by the Treasurer of
the State, with the approval of the Governor and Attorney General, in bonds of the United States or of the State of Wyoming,
or in bonds issued by school districts within this State, or registered county bonds of the State, or interest bearing warrants
of this State. The interest only shall be used for the purpose
for which the grant of lands was made.

REPEAL.

Sec. 2. Section forty of chapter seventy-nine of the Laws of 1890-91 is hereby repealed.

Approved February 16th, A. D. 1895.

CHAPTER 76.

COMPENSATION AND FEES OF COUNTY OFFICERS.

* * * * *

SUPERINTENDENTS OF SCHOOLS.

Sec. 6. County Superintendents of Schools shall receive the following annual salaries:

In counties of the first class, six hundred dollars; in counties of the second class, five hundred dollars; in counties of the third class, four hundred dollars; and in counties of the fourth class, three hundred dollars.

* * * * *

HOW PAID.

Sec. 20. The salaries of county and precinct officers as provided for in this act shall be paid in equal monthly installments, by the county in which they serve, and shall be allowed at the first regular monthly meeting of the Board of County Commissioners occurring after the rendition of such service; Provided, That in counties of the third and fourth classes the salaries of the county and precinct officers may be paid quarterly.

* * * * *

IN FORCE.

Sec. 25. This act shall take effect and be in force from and after its passage, but the same shall not affect the salary or fees of any county or precinct officer heretofore elected or appointed, during his continuance in office, pursuant to such election or appointment.

Approved February 16th, A. D. 1895.

CHAPTER 82.

STATE BOARD OF CHARITIES AND REFORM.

An Act amending and supplementing an act, approved January 8, 1891, entitled, "An act creating and establishing a State Board of Charities and Reform, and prescribing in part their duties, and repealing all acts and parts of acts inconsistent therewith."

Be it enacted by the Legislature of the State of Wyoming:

STATE ISNTITUTIONS CONTROLLED BY STATE BOARD OF CHARITIES AND REFORM.

Section 1. Sub-division two, of section two, of the act above named, is hereby amended and re-enacted so as to read as follows:

II.

General supervision and control of all buildings and institutions belonging to or used by the State for charitable, penal or reformatory purposes, including the State Insane Asylum at Evanston, in the County of Uinta; the State Penitentiary located in the town of Rawlins, in the County of Carbon; the Penitentiary located at the town of Laramie, in the County of Albany; the Deaf, Dumb and Blind Institute or Asylum located at Cheyenne, in the County of Laramie; the Wyoming General Hospital located at Rock Springs in the County of Sweetwater, and the Wyoming Soldiers' and Sailors' Home; but excepting the poor farm located at Lander, in the County of Fremont.

EXCEPTION—ANNUAL REPORT.

Sec. 2. It shall be the duty of the State Board of Charities and Reform to include in their annual report to the Governor, an itemized account of all expenditures made during the current year for the institutions under the supervision of such Board, making a complete and separate statement of the expenditures made for each of such institutions, according to the appropriation made, so that the cost of the support and maintenance of the same may be easily ascertained. They shall also include in their report in each even numbered year an itemized estimate of the amount deemed necessary by the Board to be appropriated for the support and maintenance of each of the institutions under its supervision for the ensuing two years, which estimate shall be made and itemized according to the appropriations made for the two preceding years, so that it may readily be compared with the expenditures and appropriations for those years.

SEPARATE APPROPRIATIONS.

Sec. 3. All appropriations hereafter made for the support and maintenance of the several penal, charitable and reformatory institutions under the supervision of the State Board of Charities and Reform shall state separately the amount appropriated for each institution; and it shall be the duty of the State Auditor to keep a separate account of each appropriation for the institutions, and all expenditures in connection therewith.

Sec. 4. This act shall take effect and be in force from and after its passage.

Approved February 16th, A. D. 1895.

CHAPTER 88.

INDUSTRIAL AND MANUAL TRAINING SCHOOL.

An Act permitting the School Boards to establish Industrial or Manual Training Schools.

Be it enacted by the Legislature of the State of Wyoming:

SCHOOL BOARD MAY ESTABLISH MANUAL TRAINING SCHOOLS.

Section 1. That the school board of any district in the state shall have power to establish and locate industrial and manual training schools, in connection with the public schools of said district.

Sec. 2. This Act shall take effect from and after its passage.

Approved February 18, A. D. 1895.

CHAPTER 102.

TAXATION—AMENDMENT.

An Act to amend and re-enact Sections 3768, of the Revised Statutes of Wyoming, relating to taxation.

Be it enacted by the Legislature of the State of Wyoming:

AMENDMENT.

Section 1. That section three thousand seven hundred and sixty- eight, of the Revised Statutes of Wyoming, be, and the same is hereby amended and re-enacted so as to read as follows:

ANNUAL LEVY.

'Section 3768. There shall be levied and assessed upon the taxable real and personal property. within this State in each year, the following taxes:

STATE REVENUE.

First—For State revenue, four mills on the dollar when no rate is directed by the State Board of Equalization before the date in each year when the tax ought to be levied and assessed, but in no case shall the tax for State revenue purposes exceed four mills on the dollar; except for the support of State educational and charitable institutions, the payment of the State debt and the interest thereon.

COUNTY REVENUE.

Second—The County Commissioners shall annually levy a tax for the suport of the common schools in their county, not to exceed three mills on the dollar. For county revenue for all purposes there shall be levied annually a tax, but the aggregate tax for county revenue, including general school tax, shall not exceed twelve mills on the dollar, exclusive of State revenue, except for the payment of its public debt and the interest thereon. An additional tax of two dollars for each person between the ages of twenty-one and fifty years, inclusive, shall be annually levied for county school purposes; Provided, always, That the Board of County Commissioners in each and every county of this State shall not expend in any one year, from out of the revenue so raised, for the support of the poor and lunatic purposes, a sum amounting to more than two mills on the dollar of each and every dollar of the assessed valuation of the property within their county for the then current year; for road purposes, a sum not amounting to more than three mills on the dollar of each and every dollar of assessed valuation of the property within their county for the then current year."

REPEAL

Sec. 2. All acts and parts of acts in conflict herewith, are hereby repealed.

WHEN ACT TAKES EFFECT.

Sec. 3. This act shall take effect and be in force from and after its passage.

Approved February 20th, A. D. 1895.

CHAPTER 103.

INSANE CRIMINALS.

An Act providing for the custody and treatment of persons of unsound mind who have been accused or convicted of criminal offenses.

Be it enacted by the Legislature of the State of Wyoming:

CONVICTS.

Section 1. The State Board of Charities and Reform shall make provision for the care, custody and treatment of all persons of unsound mind who are accused of, or convicted of any crime, misdemeanor, or offense against the laws of this State, or the laws of the late Territory of Wyoming, either in the State Asylum, or Hospital for the Insane at Evanston, or at a proper institution elsewhere within or without this State, after any such person of unsound mind shall be declared insane after inquiry, trial and determination as provided by law in the case of other persons of unsound mind.

RULES AND REGULATIONS.

Sec. 2. The said Board shall be empowered to make such contracts, orders, rules and regulations as shall carry into effect the provisions of this act as they may deem proper for the care, custody and treatment of the persons of unsound mind mentioned in this act.

COMPLAINT.

Sec. 3. If any person accused of or convicted of any crime, misdemeanor, or offense against the laws of this State or against the laws of the late Territory of Wyoming, shall be confined in any penitentiary, county jail of any county, or other place of confinement, awaiting trial, or who is confined therein under and pursuant to the sentence or judgment of any court or Justice of the Peace in this State, who is of unsound mind, any officer or person having such person of unsound mind in his charge shall, and any citizen of this State may, make complaint thereof, and the question of the sanity of such person shall be inquired of, tried and determined under and according to the law of this State providing for and regulating trials, inquisitions and proceeding in cases of inquiry into the sanity of other persons of unsound mind.

TRIAL OF PERSONS OF UNSOUND MIND ACCUSED OR CONVICTED OF CRIME—BOARD OF CHARITIES AND REFORM SHALL TAKE CHARGE.

Sec. 4. If any such person accused of or convicted of any crime, misdemeanor or offense shall be found of unsound mind or insane upon such inquiry, trial or proceeding, he or she shall be forthwith taken to such place or places for treatment as shall be provided for or prescribed by the State Board of Charities and Reform, either generally, or for that particular case, and it shall be the duty of any and all persons, boards, superintendents, officers and employes of the place so designated by such Board to receive the same person into custody and to treat him or her according to the regulations and practice of such place or institution.

DISPOSITION OF PERSON UPON RECOVERY OF REASON.

Sec. 5. If any such person or patient so confined in any hospital or asylum or place designated by the said Board of Charities and Reform shall recover his or her reason, he or she shall be returned to the Penitentiary, county jail or other place of confinement or imprisonment where such person was confined at the time of such inquiry, trial or proceeding to

determine his sanity or insanity, there to be tried or to serve
out or undergo his other term of imprisonment if any part
thereof remains, as the nature of the case shall require.

COSTS.

Sec. 6. The cost of the custody, maintenance, and treatment of the persons mentioned in this act at any asylum, hospital or place for the treatment and care of the insane shall
be borne by this State, and the Board of Charities and Reform
shall audit, the Auditor shall draw his warrant therefor and
the Treasurer shall pay the same in the manner provided by
law for the auditing and payment of the expenses of other
pauper insane.

WHEN ACT TAKES EFFECT.

Sec. 7. This act shall take effect immediately.
Approved February 20th, A. D. 1895.

CHAPTER 109.

REGULATION OF EXPENDITURES FOR AGRICULTURAL COL-
LEGE.

An Act regulating the appropriation, use and expenditure of
the moneys received under an act of Congress approved
March 2, 1887, entitled, "An act to establish agricultural
experiment stations in connection with the colleges established in the several States under the provisions of an act
approved July 2, 1862, and of the acts supplementary
thereto."

Be it enacted by the Legislature of the State of Wyoming:

Section 1. The moneys received under an act of Congress, approved March 2, 1887, entitled, "An act to establish
agricultural experiment stations in connection with the colleges established in the several States under the provisions
of an act approved July 2, 1862, and of the acts supplementary thereto," shall be appropriated, used and expended pursuant to the provisions of this act, and not otherwise.

APPROPRIATION, HOW EXPENDED.

Sec. 2. The Trustees of the University or College at Laramie, Wyoming, in connection with which such experimental station is established shall annually, by resolution, specifically appropriate and designate the uses to which such money shall be applied and the purposes for which the same shall be expended. Such uses and purposes at all times to be within the use and purpose for which such money is donated under the acts of Congress regulating the same, and no part of such money shall be used or expended in any manner or for any purpose not covered by such appropriation, and no indebtedness shall be contracted or expenditure made in excess of such appropriation.

TREASURER.

Sec. 3. The Treasurer of the University or College in connection with which such experimental station is established shall annually, on or before the 31st day of December submit to the Governor a printed report setting forth the appropriation resolution for that year and containing an itemized statement of the receipt and disbursement of such money, showing clearly the purposes for which the same has been expended and the amount thereof expended upon each experimental station. One hundred copies of such printed report shall be filed with the Secretary of State for distribution among the members of the Legislature and other public officers.

WHEN ACT SHALL TAKE EFFECT.

Sec. 4. This act shall take effect and be in force from and after its passage

Approved February 21st, A. D. 1895.

CHAPTER 110.

APPROPRIATIONS FOR UNIVERSITY.

An Act concerning appropriations for the support and maintenance of the University of Wyoming and requiring an annual accounting of the expenditure of the same.

Be it enacted by the Legislature of the State of Wyoming:

LEGISLATURE SHALL MAKE APPROPRIATION.

Section 1. Hereafter there shall be appropriations made by the Legislature of the moneys intended for the support and maintenance of the University of Wyoming, and such appropriations shall specify as nearly and accurately as the same can be done the specific purposes for which such moneys are intended and may be used. Such appropriations shall apply to and include all moneys received by the University from the United States for the endowment and support of colleges for the benefit of agriculture and mechanic arts, but moneys so received from the United States shall be appropriated, applied and used solely for the purpose specified in the acts of Congress regulating the same. No expenditure shall be made in excess of such appropriation and no moneys so appropriated shall be used for any purpose other than that for which they are appropriated.

TREASURER.

Sec. 2. It shall be the duty of the Treasurer of the University, immediately after the close of each current year, to submit to the Governor a printed report containing an itemized account of all moneys received for the support and maintenance of the University for that year, and of all expenditures made therefrom; and he shall at the same time file in the office of the Secretary of State, for distribution among the members of the Legislature and other public officers, one hundred copies of such report.

Sec. 3. This act shall taake effect and be in force from and after its passage.

Approved February 21st, A. D. 1895.

INDEX.

INDEX.

***

A.

B.

D.

86 · INDEX.

www.ingramcontent.com/pod-product-compliance
Lightning Source LLC
Chambersburg PA
CBHW031445270326
41930CB00007B/873